M E N

MEN:
A Translation for Women

Joan Shapiro, M.D.

In Collaboration With George Hartlaub, M.D.

A DUTTON BOOK

DUTTON
Published by the Penguin Group
Penguin Books USA Inc., 375 Hudson Street,
New York, New York 10014, U.S.A.
Penguin Books Ltd, 27 Wrights Lane, London W8 5TZ, England
Penguin Books Australia Ltd, Ringwood, Victoria, Australia
Penguin Books Canada Ltd, 10 Alcorn Avenue,
Toronto, Ontario, Canada M4V 3B2
Penguin Books (N.Z.) Ltd, 182–190 Wairau Road, Auckland 10, New Zealand

Penguin Books Ltd, Registered Offices:
Harmondsworth, Middlesex, England

First published by Dutton, an imprint of New American Library,
a division of Penguin Books USA Inc.
Distributed in Canada by McClelland & Stewart Inc.

First Printing, January, 1992
10 9 8 7 6 5 4 3 2 1

REGISTERED TRADEMARK—MARCA REGISTRADA

LIBRARY OF CONGRESS CATALOGING IN PUBLICATION DATA:
Shapiro, Joan, 1950–
    Men : a translation for women / Joan Shapiro.
        p.   cm.
    Includes bibliographical references and index.
    ISBN 0-525-93391-3
    1. Masculinity (Psychology) 2. Men—Psychology. 3. Sex
differences (Psychology) 4. Interpersonal relations.
5. Interpersonal communication. 6. Communication in marriage.
I. Title.
BF692.5.S48   1992
155.3'32—dc20
                                                    91-21659
                                                      CIP

Printed in the United States of America
Designed by Eve L. Kirch

To the men in my life:
Jack, David, and George—
father, brother, and husband

Contents

Acknowledgments

I have a number of people to thank, each of whom helped me with this book in a different way. I want to thank George Hartlaub, my husband and collaborator, whose personal insights and experiences were the impetus for this book, and whose enthusiastic editing gave me confidence. I also want to thank him for many undisturbed days and evenings. Next is Faith Hamlin, my agent. Her faith (yes!) in and excitement for this project made it a pleasure all along the way. She also taught me more than she probably is aware. Thanks also to my editor, Alexia Dorszynski, whose talent, humor, and encouragment provided immeasurable support.

I also want to thank Elynore Shapiro, Anne Ceranek, and Jacquie Carducci, whose reactions to early sketches for the book gave me confidence to pursue the project. I appreciate the input of my study group members, and especially John Graves, M.D., for many thoughtful comments. Thanks also to Ton Anders, M.D., for his skepticism and support; and to Michal Clive, for showing me how to get started. I am grateful to Sally McCain, for helping me regain my fire. Finally, I want to thank those people who must remain nameless for reasons of confidentiality, but whose stories make the book come alive.

Introduction

GETTING CLOSER

I t's Saturday. Ed is on the edge of his chair, beer in hand, glued to the TV. The announcer is explaining in excited detail "... this could just be the most important game of the season!" No fan would miss a single action-packed minute of the showdown between these two top-ranked teams. "Here's the tip-off!"

This particular Saturday is a beautiful day, late in April. The sun has been out all morning, and the day promises to be the first really warm day of the spring. Laura, Ed's wife, has gotten all of her household projects finished early and is really pleased about the prospect of spending a lovely afternoon with Ed. Maybe they'll walk downtown, or through that lovely neighborhood where the early spring bulbs are starting to bloom. They can have a cup of cappuccino at an outdoor café and have plenty of time to talk.

Laura walks into the family room and sees Ed at the TV. Sports again! Memories of many other days like this immediately fill her mind. She can predict the whole conversation that she and Ed would have if she tried to get

3

him to share the afternoon with her as she'd like: "I've worked hard all week," he would say. "I just need this one day to relax." Or, if he is in a bad mood: "Why are you pressuring me?" Or "If that's what you want to do, go ahead."

Laura is filled with loneliness, disappointment, and rage. She really loves Ed, and it is painful for her to feel that she cannot ever seem to be as interesting to him as whatever sports event is on TV. She can't get Ed to want to spend quiet, intimate time with her. She picks up the latest best-seller, gets a diet soda and a bag of potato chips, and tries to lose herself in someone else's fantasy world. Her own is too disappointing.

There must be a better way than this for Laura and Ed. She is building up a storehouse of resentment and has no tools for understanding why Ed won't connect with her. She just feels angry and hurt. Ed picks up on the anger, but can't really identify it. But it does feel uncomfortable, and he distances himself from Laura, especially when he wants to have a peaceful Saturday afternoon watching a great game and she's going to want him to do something else.

Understanding each other has got to help turn things around. It won't make Ed prefer a walk in the garden to the championship game, anymore than it will make Laura shun a sunny afternoon of quiet talking in favor of listening to the local call-in sports talk show. But it will help Ed and Laura know what is going on between them and why, in different ways, their interaction is important to both of them. It will give them options in communicating with each other and keep resentment and misunderstanding from building between them. It will help them get closer. That is what women want, and that is what this book is about.

TWO DIFFERENT WORLDS—
A CROSS-CULTURAL PERSPECTIVE

I was in China recently, in January. It was very cold in north China; the buildings were not heated, and every other person had a cough or a cold. Let me tell you how the Chinese blow their noses. (Keep reading this, now, it's important.) They put a finger over one nostril to block it, and they blow hard through the other nostril, and whatever comes out hits the sidewalk. Of course I found this disgusting! But then I spoke with some American friends who were teaching in China. They had something very interesting to say about this. What they explained was that the Chinese think that to blow your nose into a piece of paper, fold it up, then put it in your purse and *save* it is utterly repulsive! And it certainly is! How different things can look when you are from another culture!

To try to understand more about men, think about it as a visit to a foreign country. When you visit a new country, you have to learn about a new language, new customs, a new history, a new sense of values. Things aren't automatically bad because they are different, but they often seem to be. Human beings have a characteristic response to an outside culture: we think that it is wrong. Or that it is silly, or stupid, sacrilegious, naïve, or evil. That's how we think. So as we enter this new territory, this foreign culture of men, we are likely to have this response: "Why would he want to do a thing like that?" Or "Anyone with common sense would know ..." Any *woman* with common sense might know, but not a man, because he grew up in a foreign, in a different culture. But if we are going to get along better with someone who is different from us, the more we understand about him, the better. There's just no doubt about it.

WHAT THIS BOOK WILL DO

But haven't we *always* been trying to understand men? We wish they would try to understand us for a change. Why should we have to read another book that will help us have better relationships? Isn't it their turn to do some reading?

The reality is that we as women do most of this kind of work of trying to understand. As Jean Baker Miller so clearly explains in her book *Toward a New Psychology of Women*, women and men behave as members of any subordinate and dominant cultures do. In this framework, the dominant culture is the group with the power, prestige, control, property, and value. The subordinate culture is the group that is without power or control, that is devalued, and that depends, therefore, on the good will of the dominant group for well-being and even survival. Men, who are the dominant culture in most societies, have little need to understand the subordinate culture, while women, as the subordinate culture, *must* understand the dominant culture—it is important for survival.

Harvard psychologist Carol Gilligan in *In a Different Voice*, as well as others, has clearly described how we as women learn to care about and care for relationships. In her work, Gilligan has shown how boys make decisions based on following rules, or getting clear results, whereas girls make decisions based on how others feel, or on what it takes to maintain a sense of harmony in relationships. Concern about relationships, then, is an important part of our self-concept as women. So it is not surprising that we pay attention to, and try to learn about, what the other person is like.

This interest notwithstanding, I think we have spent a lot of time and energy in complaining about men and not as much in trying to really understand them. In our relationship with men, our understanding is colored by negative value judgments and criticism. This book can make a difference for women because it is a sympathetic portrait of the world of men and of their experience in it. After all, most women care about men, and an awful lot of us choose to live with men. We want to be happy doing so, if we can.

This book is about the men who really do intend to get along with us, even if they do not know how to do it very well. They are the men who are well-intentioned, if inept, who are good-hearted, though insensitive, who consider themselves open-minded, though they may be uninformed.

It is not about sadistic, aggressive men who really do not care about women as people, who actively hurt and disparage women. It is not written as a way to learn to deal better with those men who do not have our best interests at heart, although there are books written to help women deal with these men, such as *Men Who Hate Women and the Women Who Love Them*, by Susan Forward, or *Women Who Love Too Much*, by Robin Norwood. Women who are involved with such men do need help learning how to deal with or get out of those relationships, and these books as well as helping professionals can help them address these serious issues. But this book is not about those relationships or those men. It is about all men, to some extent, but mostly about the decent men who really like women, whom we try to get along with, and who want to be happy with us.

I am not ignoring the many horrible things women have suffered and continue to suffer at the hands of men. I could offer psychological explanations for those things if I wanted to. I don't want to. I am not interested in offering reasons for cruel or selfish behavior. I will not give justifications for unacceptable behavior, and I will not grant women more permission to accept such behavior. We already have enough of that.

I have written this book from the perspective of someone who is part of a broader culture: a mostly middle-class, mostly white, Western, first-world society. There are many aspects of other cultures that do not fit my descriptions and explanations. Different dynamics will apply in different cultures. I recognize this, but I am choosing not to make this fact a focus of this book. Despite differences, anthropologists have found some interesting similarities across cultures, most notably that manhood is a state to be fought for and achieved. I do think that this concept does apply, though in different forms, for many people. But I will focus on the one perspective I am familiar with, and I believe that this makes the points I want to make clear and specific.

This book contains generalizations and even stereotypes. The purpose of these generalizations is not to suggest that everyone will fit into these categories, because every human being is distinct and has his or her own personal history. The purpose of these descriptions is to reveal the patterns that do exist in our culture. These cultural realities have a profound impact on all of us as individuals. So even though each individual is unique, there are certain forces that affect all of us.

This is not a how-to book about making men be more like women. It is not a book about changing men. After all, we don't have power to change other people. We only have power to change ourselves, including how we relate to, think, and feel about others. So we can learn how to communicate more effectively with men, and we can learn to distinguish the things men unintentionally do that hurt us from deliberate cruelty. We can learn how men think about themselves and about us as women. We can learn what their struggles and dreams are like; we can learn what pressures they feel. These things will all change how we relate to men. But we can't change ourselves in our relationship with men unless we understand them. And that is what this book is about.

WHY I CAN PROVIDE THIS TRANSLATION

Perhaps without realizing it at first, I have always been a little bit "bi-lingual." I grew up with a twin brother. Twins are usually close, and we certainly were. Before my brother learned that he was supposed to keep his distance from me because I was a girl, I got to learn a lot about his experience, just by being so close to him. So on an unconscious and pre-verbal level, as well as from regular experience, I think I've always had a kind of feel for the world of men.

Another credential is that I am married to a wonderful and sensitive man who has shared openly about himself and who has been teaching me his language. He has had the courage to show me his inner world and the world that he shares with other men. He is a gifted psychoanalyst and has shared his knowledge and experience as a therapist, as well as his own experiences as a man. Many of the ideas in this book are his or are ideas we have developed together. This book literally would not be possible without him.

My third credential is that I am a therapist. The women, men, couples, and families that I have seen in fourteen years of clinical practice have also taught me about men and women. As I have developed the ideas in this book, my work with men and with couples has been transformed. When I understand men from the perspectives in this book, they feel really understood. When I can translate men to the women they are involved with, relationships flourish. Some of the men and women with whom I have worked may recognize themselves in these pages, though they are disguised. They have read and agreed to the publication of these disguised versions of their stories. I am grateful for what I have learned from them.

I have also learned from the students I have taught, together with my husband, about the psychology of men and women. I learn something new in every class I teach. Out of one of these classes developed an ongoing study group about men and women. In this mixed group of therapists, we have each been able to be a "fly on the wall," able to hear what the "other side" really thinks. We have developed considerable trust in each other over the years and have all been enlightened about each other.

What I have learned has been fascinating, funny, scary at times, and promising. These ideas work. My patients have clearly benefited from them. My best evidence that these ideas work is the profoundly satisfying relationship I have with my husband. My hope is that they help many others as well.

Chapter One

SOLDIER

My husband kills the bugs in our house. I don't think I am unusually squeamish, and we did not have a discussion about whose job it should be to get rid of nasty-looking creatures. All that happened was that I would say, "Ooh, what a big, awful spider!" and before I could even look around for a shoe or a newspaper, my husband would be there, tissue in hand, removing the offending bug without a noise or complaint. What I found out a short time later is that he absolutely hates bugs; he is quite squeamish and would rather not have to look at, let alone touch, insects. But he does it because he sees it as his job. He perfected his talent while he was raising his children. He didn't want them to be frightened. And he especially didn't want his sons to see his fear, since he wanted them to be more "manly" than he was, and since he knew that there wasn't "really" anything to be afraid of.

Before I got shut out of the world of boys, as all girls do, I got an intense glimpse of it. I remember one particular day very clearly, a day that made me realize how different my life was going to be from a boy's, and from my brother's. My brother, my father, and I were going for a walk. We (since my brother is my twin, it has always been "we," not "I") were about eight years old. My brother was asking my father questions about joining the army. Would he have to go? How old would he be? Would there be a war? Would he have to fight? I remember feeling very far away emotionally. As they talked, I knew that their conversation would not ever include me. For the first time, I was glad. I didn't want to be drafted and go to war, and I knew I would never have to. I felt guilty, frightened for my brother, but relieved for myself. I would dream, every now and then, after that discussion, that I was a soldier in battle. I would always turn and run. And I could always wake up from this nightmare and know that it was only a dream. My brother would never be able to have that same kind of relief.*

Fred had had a heart attack, his first, and a relatively mild one, in his mid-fifties. Two months later, the first heavy snowfall arrived. Maddy, his wife, woke up the morning after the storm to find Fred already out of bed. She put on her slippers and robe and went to the kitchen expecting to find him drinking coffee and reading the morning paper. But she didn't find coffee made or Fred inside the house. She heard a scraping noise and looked outside. There was Fred, shoveling the snow to clear the

---

*And though women have now been involved in combat, they did so as part of an all-volunteer army; they had not been drafted and were not obliged to serve.

driveway. She asked him to come in. "Just as soon as I finish clearing this path so we can get our cars out," he said. Maddy tried to get him to come inside, but he resisted. When he finally came in, she asked why they couldn't have waited until someone came around offering to shovel. "It had to be done," said Fred. "I've got important meetings today at work. I've got to be there." "Even if it kills you," thought Maddy.

Men are expected to be like soldiers all the time, and they come to expect this of themselves. They act brave and take charge even if others, including we women, don't overtly ask them to do so. If there is a noise in the house in the middle of the night, the man is expected to get up to investigate, even if he has no knowledge of self-defense. "Women and children first" is the familiar phrase. That means "Men last." When the *Titanic* was sinking, the women and children were put in lifeboats, but the men and adolescent boys were left behind to go down with the ship. Uncomplaining. Men are not supposed to expect anything different from this. They are to be strong and brave, no matter what the cost. And being strong and brave means doing what needs to be done, without showing any feelings.

MEN ARE THE ONES WHO GO TO WAR

Understanding the metaphor of the soldier goes far in helping you understand men. That they are the ones who go to war is invisibly woven into the fabric of men's lives.

It is an inevitable consequence of being born male. For all of recorded history, when there has been a war, men have fought.

The very ways that we raise boys and the attitudes and values surrounding their existence mold the male character to be ready for the military and for war. We all have very specific cultural expectations that are different for girls and for boys. Girls are supposed to be sweet, soft, gentle, and relatively well-behaved. They are also considered to be relatively weak, helpless, and in need of protection. Boys are supposed to be rough, tough, loud, and dirty. They are also expected to be strong and not to show any sign of weakness.

My husband, who has taught me most of what I know about men's real inner sensitivity, was playing with his eighteen-month-old grandson recently. They were having a grand old time together, until the toddler tripped and bumped his head on a table. Before he knew what was happening, my husband said, he found himself thinking of telling this small child that it didn't really hurt, that he shouldn't cry, to be a big boy. He quickly caught himself, comforted his little grandson, and kissed his boo-boo. He was both glad that he had been aware enough to make the shift and amazed at how automatic these cultural responses are. We *all* seem to expect boys to be brave little soldiers. The anticipation of being a soldier is so much a part of the boy's psyche that he literally "grows up fighting." The emphasis on competitive sports is just one example of the power and pervasiveness of this training.

It's no wonder, then, that boys grow up with the awareness that they will be soldiers and develop an unconscious
and sometimes a conscious belief that they must be prepared to fight the enemy. Whether they actually enter the
service, or dodge the draft, or live in a time of relative
peace when few boys are called, this is still part of the
boy's awareness. Deep inside, therefore, they learn to be
ready at any moment to fight.

According to Vamik Volkan, a psychoanalyst and director
of the Center for the Study of the Mind and Human Interaction, there is a universal psychological need to have enemies and allies. Dr. Volkan has written persuasively that in
the course of becoming a separate person and developing
an individual identity, each person has a sense of other
groups of people not only as "not like me," but also as
"alien" and as "enemy." Wars are fought largely with these
beliefs. We believe that the enemy we fight and kill is not
like us. He is inferior, ignorant, evil, deranged, subhuman.
During World War II, for example, the Japanese were
"slant-eyed monkeys" and the Germans were "barbarian
huns." In Vietnam we fought the "godless communists";
the cold war was a conflict with the "evil empire."

Men are the ones who fight this enemy. Yet the beliefs
about the enemy are cultural and universal. We all—male
and female, young and old—have them. We make the for-
eigner distinct from us so that we can feel clearer about
ourselves. Our boys who fight, then, are sacrificed, they
fight and die, to maintain a universal, human developmental need.

There are many ways in which men behave, think, feel,

and relate to others that are a part of battle-readiness. Men are well acquainted with this experience, but women are not. We have to push ourselves to think about what it would be like to know that we are the ones who go to war. When we do, we find that this does not feel good. But we have to think about it in order to understand men, because it does not feel good to them either, yet has always been their reality.

As boys grow up they learn that they may be expected to leave their homes, families, and all the things that are important to them in order to join the army, perhaps never to return. They will be trained for going to war. In this training a man who is a complete stranger will give them orders about everything they say and do. They will learn to obey him without question because this is a crucial part of being prepared to go into battle. They must be prepared to take up their weapons and march toward the enemy, who has his weapons, too. These young boys are being trained to follow orders to march into battle, knowing that when they do they may be killed. They must be ready to watch their friends die because they know that in war, death is a reality. But they must follow orders and they must march forward nonetheless.

This is the kind of responsibility and pressure that we women must make ourselves think about as we work to understand men better. Men cannot let themselves feel frightened because they cannot turn and run: that is against everything they have been trained to do, against orders, against the rules. And it is contrary to *who* they have been raised to be—that is, it threatens the very basic inner sense of self. "Coward" is one of the worst things that a boy or a man can be called.

These lessons are learned in childhood, during the time that we generally absorb our culture's values, standards, and morals. Culture is transmitted largely by other children. Here is where and when boys begin to learn the lessons of war and how to be a soldier. The correct behavior is handed down from those who are only slightly older, but who have just learned the rules. In the absence of a strong, available model, boys will follow their peers' behavior, which often is an exaggerated, macho version of masculinity. The rules here are strict, adherence to them is required, and breaking them almost surely makes one an outcast. To be one of the boys, one of the gang, a boy must learn to keep a stiff upper lip (no quivering as in crying), to keep his chin up (proud and brave), to suck it up (get that scared, sinking feeling out of the pit of your stomach), to be a soldier.

HOW IT FEELS TO BE A SOLDIER

How do you run your life, and how do you experience day-to-day living when you know that you may have to lose it all at any moment, and do so as if voluntarily, without complaint? What do you do with your wants, needs, plans, hopes, dreams, and commitments? If you think about it, if you really put yourself in this spot and feel what it is like, being a solider is an inherently painful position. Intolerable, in fact. In order to function, you have to insulate yourself from your feelings. You would lose your mind if you actually lived every day knowing that you might have to relinquish everything at any moment. Your caring, your attachment, your intense connections would have to be protected. Your feelings would be hidden from other people, but mostly they would be hidden from yourself.

Picture watching a war movie with this familiar dialogue:

> "We've got to take this hill."
> "Not much chance that more than half of us will make it back, and you know it, sir."
> "Yes, but if we don't move forward now, they'll think our strength is dwindling, and they'll be right. If they launch a major offensive, a lot more guys will die. We have to move forward. We have no choice."
> "Right, sir. I'll begin briefing the men."

If you think about yourself as one of these soldiers, you realize that you can't run up a hill firing a gun at the enemy with shots aimed at you and *feel* what is happening. If you did, wouldn't you just turn and run back down the hill, as I did in my nightmares? Something must insulate you from the terror or you wouldn't fight and wouldn't survive.

One of the most difficult things for us all to do is to empathize with something we never have to experience. It is not uncommon for a man to faint in a delivery room because he is unprepared to see so much blood or because it is too painful for him to watch his wife in the agony of labor. Similarly, although we are learning about what it is like to be a man at work, we as women tend to avoid thinking about what a man might have to do to himself in order to go to war. This is one of the areas in which women avoid empathizing with men. We can say that their behavior is unnecessary or foolish. We can say that old men perpetuating wars that young men have to fight is outrageous. But the young men still have to go. So they have to deal with the emotional consequences of this, whether we like it or not. (And we have to deal with the emotional consequences of this, whether *we* like it or not.) They have to constrict, control, and insulate themselves. To be men, men have to not feel.

To be more specific, it is their own personal and vulnerable feelings that men cannot feel. There are, however, a few feelings that they can have. They can take pride in their country, in their leaders, and especially in their unit, their team. They can (and must!) have confidence in their own skill. They can hate the enemy. They can have a great deal of anger, which gets mobilized into life-saving action. But it would be impossible for them to function as soldiers if they had doubts and fears, wished to be back home, questioned their leaders, or worried about the feelings of the enemy.

Because of how difficult it is to annihilate another person, men have learned to dehumanize the "other." Then a man does not have to deal with the human interaction. He doesn't have to be restricted by the complications of feelings about the other person. He just has to do the job.

And he feels good about getting the job done. That is really all that counts.

Sometimes, in life, it is the woman who is the enemy. A woman is alien, "other," and therefore threatening. She comes from another world, a world whose customs, traits, and beliefs are radically different from anything masculine. Men avoid getting involved in this world at all costs, because to do so threatens the laboriously achieved status of being a man. When a man feels in conflict with a woman, he can, and often must, insulate himself from her as he does from the enemy. The feeling and the connection are gone. Once she has been dehumanized, she can be shut out and she is not as threatening. The man can go about his business without emotional interference. There will be more in chapter 2 about how a woman gets to be so threatening. But for now, it is useful to realize that a man's reaction to a woman may be as if he is at war, and she is the feared (yes, feared) enemy.

This ability to dehumanize the enemy is very important. Only a little has been written about how devastating and even disorganizing to the personality it is when a man realizes that the "enemy" is just a person. Soldiers returned from the war in Vietnam with many such stories. One talked about coming face to face with the enemy in the jungle. He looked at his adversary and realized that this was just a boy, barely eighteen. Just a boy, and a boy wearing a rosary. What did he do? He killed the boy. But then he didn't know how to deal with this. When he realized that his enemy was actually just another person, he found himself outside the system of no-feelings. And he didn't know what to do with the feelings that he had. Dehumanizing the enemy and numbing himself to his feelings were what enabled him to function. Seeing the enemy as just another person and feeling his feelings about killing this person threw him into an emotional crisis.

The ways in which men adapt to their traumatic reality are the ways in which humans adapt to and react to trauma in general. To understand this, we can think of children who are abused. How do they face the unthinkable? How do they live from day to day when they don't know if they will be safe or not? They split off the reality from their awareness. They are both there and not there at the same time. They do what we call "dissociate." That is, though they may be physically present, they are mentally somewhere else. They dis-associate their thoughts from their feelings. It is as if the painful event isn't really happening to them. Children often deny the reality of the traumatic event (and often cannot even remember its ever happening). They normalize the abuse. They don't think about it as something that is wrong or painful, but rather that it is something that happens to everyone and that simply must be endured.

What do children say when they are asked how they feel about these painful events? They deny that they feel anything. They deny that anything important has happened. They say they don't know what you are talking about even if they do. They turn away from you and play. They make jokes.

They cannot face the reality. The pain is too enormous to tolerate. And this is what men do in the face of their painful reality. They deny that it is a problem. They make a game of it. They split off the painful feelings from their awareness. They become numb.

SOLDIERS IN EVERYDAY LIFE

I was hiking with my husband in a national forest early one evening. We thought we would climb a short distance to a ridge from which we would be able to see several mountain ranges and perhaps the sunset. This was our first hike in almost a year, and it was a special one. My husband had suffered a mild heart attack six months earlier, and we didn't know how well he would do with this challenge.

As we began climbing, I noticed what looked at first like hoof prints; horses did in fact use this trail. But as we walked on, I realized that they weren't exactly like hoof prints. They sank awfully deep into the trail. As I looked more closely, I thought I saw four or five lines at the top of each print. Claws. Paws.

"Honey, I think these are bear tracks."

"Where?"

"Here."

"No, those are hoof prints. I don't think those are bear tracks," he said.

I commented on the tracks and worried about them for some time. The prints got more and more distinct, and I could see the claw marks very clearly. The bear's paws had slid on the wet trail and had left clear markings in the dried mud. I must have commented on these tracks about half a dozen times, and each time my husband said that they couldn't be bear tracks. Eventually he said that he remembered that some friends of his did go bear-hunting near here. Finally, he agreed that these probably were bear tracks. But they were old.

As we were almost back to our car, my husband picked up a very large rock and threw the rock onto the trail as hard as he could. I asked what he was doing, and he said, "This is what I hoped I could have done to that bear." Later that evening, he told me that he had been a little bit apprehensive and extra alert during the hike. In fact, he had had an elaborate plan of how he would try to protect me and us from the bear that he kept reassuring me did not exist. And in this elaborate plan, he was my protector. He did not even have to decide. The plan would have been for him to distract the bear so that I could find a safe place to hide.

He had to do it. He would be the soldier. Despite the fact that he was actually more physically vulnerable than I was, he was prepared to carry out his role. He would fight. It was expected. He expected it of himself. He didn't really question the proposition at all.

Since little boys are already beginning to prepare for this role, the model of the strong soldier who is tough and unemotional is a useful one to follow. Boys don't play with baby dolls who need gentle nurturing; they play with toy soldiers that they can arrange in battle formation. The soldiers kill and die as part of the game. The little boys can imagine themselves as soldiers in battle, sometimes as the ones who kill, and sometimes as the ones who die.

(Of course, in this game, the dead soldiers always come back to life. This particular war is not real.) The boys can begin to become desensitized, in a way, to the trauma. They can master the experience. It's a game they are playing, this killing and dying, and they are familiar with it. They don't sound frightened.

The acceptance of the reality of war and the requirement to participate in it become part of personality structure. Not-feeling becomes a part of identity, an integral part of the self, something that is automatic, not something thought about and decided anew each time. If young men get called for the draft, they are not surprised. In a way, they have always been preparing for this. When my husband knew that there might be a bear, he prepared to fight it. He did not include me in the responsibility for defending ourselves, and he did not question whether or not he could handle it himself. He was simply ready to do whatever was necessary, himself, without considering the cost. Actually, he said, he had started to be aware of the cost, but then blocked it from his mind, so that he would be able to plan and to act.

The military attitude is never far away, even for young boys. Boy Scouts, and even the Cub Scouts are junior soldiers. In their oath they swear to "do my duty to God and my country, to help other people at all times." And the motto is "Be prepared." A boy, training to be a man, learns to be everlastingly toned up for the unexpected. My husband, in preparing to fight the bear, was just "doing his duty."

As men are prepared for war, they have to train out of

themselves the tendency to feel. They have been learning not to notice feelings of fear and uncertainty. In the process of training themselves out of the *tendency* to feel, they usually train themselves out of the *capacity* to feel, as well

EMPATHY—FEELING ANOTHER'S FEELINGS

Empathy is the ability to feel with another, the ability to put yourself in someone else's shoes and imagine how she or he might be feeling. In order to do this, a person must be able to draw from his or her own experience of feelings, because it is from these feelings that we can identify and understand the other person's experience. Once we are in touch with the feeling, then we can have a much deeper understanding of the other person's experience. We can resonate with the other person, and we can often find words with which to express this understanding. The other person then knows that we have connected with and have understood him or her. Our knowledge of ourself, especially of our feelings, is crucial to understanding the feelings of the other person.

Since men have learned from boyhood to ignore this kind of information about themselves, they find it very difficult to feel for another person. Men are often criticized for their inability to empathize. But this ability has been trained out of them as it is trained out of all good soldiers. Men often are called insensitive, callous, and self-centered. And in fact, they *are* calloused. This callousness is an inevitable consequence of their role, developed because that role is traumatizing. And it is, in a sense, a requirement of that role; in order to be able to perform properly, a soldier cannot let himself feel. Although this is frustrating for women, it is not generally distressing for men. In fact, men get on well with other men because none of them is expected to show feelings. In a way, by their socialization, all men are somewhat like army buddies.

This lack of feeling may sound like an exaggeration. It is also something that women don't want to hear. We don't want to have our worst fears confirmed: that men can't feel. We are frustrated with men because they don't seem to understand us or our feelings. We are disappointed that they don't share their feelings. We get angry at men when the answer to the question "What are you feeling?" is "Nothing." We get angry because we think men are withholding. Obviously, we think, they must be feeling something and they're just not telling us.

But it is understandable that men do not feel. It is normal for them to be relatively numb for all the reasons we have described. As is often the case, necessity has become a virtue. In fact, in the culture of men, a stoic and emotionless demeanor is a highly prized characteristic. Think of John Wayne's blank face at the threat of danger, Clint Eastwood saying, "Make my day," Bruce Willis in *Die Hard*, or any male actor in films. Or think of your local TV news and notice how seldom men show feeling. That very lack of emotion is the paragon of masculine virtue.

We, as women, have an agenda for men: we want them to change, to be more sensitive, more emotional, to show more feelings. But why should they? What good would it do them? They would have to have all those painful feelings and yet still get the job done. (I don't think many women would be particularly pleased if their husbands started saying things like, "I feel too overwhelmed by sadness today. I can't go to work. I hope I don't get fired for not finishing the year-end report.") We want men to be more sensitive, but we don't want them to fall down on the job!

And then, of course, a man doesn't want his buddies to see that he's "sensitive." He's likely to be teased about it and experience his sense of himself as a man as being at risk. When men show feelings of sadness, or show tears when talking, they almost always say "I'm sorry," as if they shouldn't.

There is a lot of pressure on men to stay just the way they are. It is only with sufficient motivation and in a very safe and trusting relationship that a man is able to change his efficient and stoic soldier stance to one of an open and sensitive man. After all, why should he change? His role hasn't changed. If there's danger of an intruder, he has to investigate. If the car has a flat tire in a snowstorm, he still has to go outside and change it. If there is some large, repulsive, unidentifiable insect in the bathtub, he is still the one who has to get rid of it. If the ship is sinking, he still has to go down with it. With these demands, why should he want to have a lot of feelings?

Thus, a man must overcome a tremendous amount of internal resistance and downright ignorance in order to be more open, more vulnerable to a woman, to the "other." And yet men really do want to please women. They just don't know how. Sadly, they often don't realize how important this kind of emotional openness is to women until they are threatened with separation or divorce. One of the reasons why a man might want to change is to maintain a relationship with a woman.

In addition, if he feels permission to let go of any parts of his traditional role, then the requirement for him to be unfeeling may be less stringent. He might have some option, then, to think and feel differently. He might have the safety and freedom to begin to value and be aware of feelings. After he reaches that point, it will take an enormous amount of practice for him to *learn* to feel. At this point, he does not have a whole set of feelings, fully formed and ready to be expressed when the circumstances are right. And unfortunately, it may not be possible for the man to reveal his feelings even though blocks are removed. He will have to start from scratch, learning how to feel. He will have to learn to do something that, up until this point, he has learned *not* to do.

He will have to take the delicate beginnings of feelings that he has experienced and let them grow. He has learned to push them down and stamp them out without thought and often without awareness. Now he must value, nurture, and develop them and then—horror of horrors—*show* them. He will feel exposed. He will be vulnerable. For him, his very self, his life, will be endangered. He needs to be nurtured through these vulnerable periods. If you tell him, for example, "Thank you for letting me know you feel that way. It helps me understand you better, and makes me feel better about how this affects us," you are going to encourage more of this same behavior. However, if you say something like, "It's about time you owned up to that," it may well be the last time you hear about these feelings.

The metaphor of the soldier helps us understand that men are ready for war at all times. They are armored against danger, loss, and death. In order for them to be able to feel, then, they must feel safe. They must be able to feel that they are *not* on the brink of going into battle. For although the war they are preparing to fight may be imaginary, their stance of readiness is real. It is a generalized response to all dangers, great and small. It is a response to danger perceived by men, and it is a response that is supported and valued by everyone, men and women, who want men to be strong.

It is shocking and painful to find out that we, as women, trigger many of these feelings of danger. We are alien, other—we are the enemy. It's easy to see someone else as foreign or different, but difficult to remember that that is often how we appear to others. Also, we have been trained to believe in our cultural roles: society as a whole sees women as "lesser," and so we rarely think of ourselves as powerful or dangerous. And yet to men, that is exactly what we are.

Traditional roles maintain the status quo in our society. But they aren't the whole reality. They are only the visible structure that, for better and worse, stabilizes the fabric of society and organizes our daily lives. Behind this visible structure lie other, more complicated, and often more painful feelings.

Let me add a note here about external and internal reality. We all have shared ideas and beliefs, values and goals. Then we have our inner emotional life, which is private, and, in some sense, sheltered from the real world. Our internal reality is not always in agreement with our external reality. Changes in our inner world usually lag behind external changes, which means that changes in social structure are not always mirrored in internal thoughts and feelings.

I had a startling experience of this during my pregnancy. Although I had thought that I was carrying a boy, after amniocentesis I found out that I was actually carrying a girl. As I felt more and more fetal movement, I was shocked to find myself thinking that so much activity would be acceptable behavior for a little boy. But it felt like a girl should be more gentle and peaceful. In my professional life, I am a feminist. I co-founded a therapy center for women. I don't actually *believe* what I felt. My inner world is lagging behind everything that I think and believe. It is difficult to erase what we have been taught— that women should be kinder, gentler, less antagonistic, and men more powerful and assertive.

In reality, although we are considered "lesser" by culture and society, we as women have a lot of power over men, and we often make them feel as if they are in great emotional danger. They hide this, of course, from themselves as well as from us and go on feeling and looking like good soldiers. It appears as though nothing is bothering them at all when, in fact, they are quite vulnerable to us. We all tend to be swayed by the picture of the controlled, harsh, and distant exterior. But we miss what is inside.

We can have some impact in this area if we understand more about it. We will get a clearer picture of men's fear of us as we go on to look at what men, throughout their lives, learn to feel about women.

Chapter Two

MOTHER

The night before Stan's wedding, amidst all the flurry of activity and the preparations for the rehearsal dinner, Stan's mother managed to pull him aside.

"Now, you've been a wonderful son, and I know you'll be a wonderful husband. But I want you to realize that you can't expect any woman, including Ellen, ever to do all the things for you that I did."

Denise was involved in her usual pre-holiday chores, keeping track of all the necessary tasks as she kept busy attending to them. She called to Irv, who was in another room.

"Did you take the garbage out yet?" She wanted to know because she had some things that she wanted him to take out with him.

"You told me you wanted me to finish paying the bills!"

Denise, not knowing what the bills had to do with garbage, said, "Well, that's right, but I have some things to go out, and I just wondered if you would be able to take them out before you go."

"I can't do everything at once. I wish you would just make up your mind."

Denise joined Irv in his office. "What's wrong? You sound pretty upset."

"I'm not upset. I'm just tired of your criticizing everything I do. I do one thing that you want, and you criticize me because I'm not doing something else! You're always on top of me for everything. Will you just back off? I feel like I can't win."

Meg and Phil came home from a lively dinner party at the home of some good friends. As they were getting ready for bed, Meg decided to confront Phil with what had been bothering her most of the evening.

"You seemed to be paying an awful lot of attention to Tracy tonight."

"No, I wasn't."

"Well, it seemed to me that you always focused the conversation on her; you laughed at her silly jokes; you just seemed to enjoy her a lot."

"You're nuts. I don't know how you end up with these ideas. It was a great party, and I was having a good time. You're just too sensitive, especially about how you look. Why don't you stop nursing Josh so you can lose the rest of that weight? Then you'll feel better."

"Don't blame this one on me. Why can't you take responsibility for your own actions? Why must you lie to me?"

"I can only tell you the truth as I see it," said Phil, as he thought to himself, "Dammit, I enjoy another woman

at a party and I have to watch whether I smile 'too much'
or have 'too much' fun. That's not flirting! Well, maybe it
is. Hell, I don't know!"

Alan is in therapy only because of Julie's insistence. But
now that he's there, he has plenty to say.

"She has something to say about everything I do. 'You
don't make enough money.' 'You watch too much TV.' 'You
never think of things for us to do together.' 'You treat me
like I'm an afterthought or an irritation in your life.' "

Julie an afterthought? From working with Alan I knew
that nothing could be farther from the truth. "But she is
the most important thing in your life, isn't she?" I said.

Still agitated, Alan confided quietly, "That's why it hurts
so much. If she thinks I'm okay, then I am. If she doesn't
like me, then I'm nothing. I feel dead inside, like I can't
say or do anything. Every time she disapproves of me, I
know she thinks I'm a nobody. So I am a nobody. Why
does she want to do this to me? Why doesn't she like me?
I'm not that bad."

What's wrong with these guys? Why are they so sensitive?
Why do they get so hurt when we are talking about *our*
pain? Why do they get so defensive, so quickly? Amazingly
enough, it has a lot to do with some painful and inevitable
consequences of a son's being raised by a mother. These
consequences do not occur because anybody did anything
wrong; they just happen because of the way life is.

To get back to Alan, I am certainly sympathetic to Alan's
pain. I know that he is hurt, angry, frustrated, and con-

fused. He is trying so hard to please Julie, yet she never seems to be satisfied. Since he is in therapy, I can work with him to help him feel better about himself so that he is not so easily knocked down by Julie's comments. But I find myself thinking about Julie, too. After all, I'm a lot more like Julie than I am like Alan! I know how she feels. And I'm pretty sure that she doesn't feel that she criticizes Alan all the time. She is probably proud that, when she has something to say, she is assertive enough to say it out loud instead of letting it fester inside her. From her point of view, she is just expressing herself.

Part of me feels like saying, "So *big deal*, Alan. Be a man! Julie's only another person, saying what she thinks. If you don't agree with her, just say so. Everything she says couldn't be *that* important. Grow up!"

I feel this way because I know that, as a woman, I don't feel very important. Most of the women I know have similar feelings. We have always been devalued, in many areas of life. We are seen as less intelligent and powerful than men. We don't earn the same money as men for the same work. "Women's work" (child care, homemaking, caretaking) is trivialized, unpaid, or underpaid. Our sexuality is exploited, degraded, and devalued. We clean up after everybody. We certainly don't feel powerful or important!

In addition, the cultural stereotype is that our worth lies only in our relationship with a man. Up until recently, women's prestige was derived only from men's. According to this model, *he* is the one with the intelligence and power, so *he* is the one who should be able to make all the important decisions. *He* should have the strength to protect us from danger and fear. Our jobs, many women were taught, were to facilitate his career, to provide him with a family, and to make his life comfortable. In exchange for this, we were entitled to support and safety, and in this, we were told, we should find our success and fulfillment.

Though huge numbers of women (and men) don't believe this anymore, it was a truth to most of our parents. It colors our past . . . and our present. It is not yet solidly in place in our hearts and minds that women are as important as men. So it is very difficult, perhaps impossible, to believe that for a man, the sun may rise and set on what we say and do. How can someone as unimportant as I be the center of the universe? I'm not even the center of my own universe, let alone somebody else's, especially a man's!

But it's true. And as hard as it is to believe, as much as we don't want to think this is so, Alan, in a way, is not a man. *Inside*, he often *feels* like a small boy. And most of the times that he feels the smallest, most vulnerable, and weakest are when he is with Julie. To him, Julie has all the power of a mother, and a big mother compared to a small boy at that. How angry it makes us when we women realize that the person who has so much power over us and who is supposed to protect us with that power instead acts so small and helpless. This man, the one with all the status, weight, and privilege, is vulnerable to *us*. It looks like he needs us to take care of him, but then who will take care of us?

The vulnerability that Alan feels in relation to Julie is

the same as the vulnerability he felt in relation to his mother when he was small. To understand this aspect of men, we must begin by understanding what it is like to be a little boy growing up. There will be four key points for us to look at.

The first concept that helps us make sense out of this is that the boy is raised by someone (a female) who is different than he is (a male). This is a pivotal issue in the boy's development. The boy must learn most of what he is supposed to be like from women, especially his mother, because that is who is there taking care of him. Being raised by someone who is like you and whom you can be like (as it is for us as women) is a very different experience from being raised by someone who is different from you. For the boy, it affects the whole way he learns to feel about himself, the way he learns to identify who he is.

The next important factor to consider is that in all cultures, boys are raised differently than girls are. This adds to a boy's difficulty because of the many ways he must be different from his mother, his sister, and usually his teacher. In the first few years of his life, the boy spends the great majority of his time with women, whether his mother, his grandmother, or his preschool teacher. And as the boy is learning how to be a male, he is receiving concrete messages about how he is supposed to be, messages that we see reflected later in the adult man.

Think about the mother as the key person in the small boy's life. She is, by definition, the center of everything. She can make the world a sunny place or a dungeon. So, the third point to think about is that for the rest of his life, the man will transfer this feeling onto other women. He will tend to experience them as the ones who can free or chain him.

Finally, we need to examine the consequences of the relative unavailability of the father. Here is this small boy who realizes that he is not like his mother, but is supposed to be a little man, like his father is a big man. But his father is usually so distant that the boy has real trouble figuring out what that means. The clearest thing about a father is that he goes away—to work, to his shop, to the golf course, the yard, or the TV. This early lack of male connection leads to difficulties in having a firm masculine identity, a clear and solid sense of himself as a person, a male person, with no necessity to "prove" it.

In fact, all these factors together contribute to the boy's difficulty in establishing a solid sense of himself as male. He has had to try to learn, from the very beginning, how to be himself from women, who are very different than he is. It's almost like trying to learn one language from someone who speaks another. In addition, women remain a powerful force in the man's life, and the man develops many ways both to gain access to and to protect himself from this power.

This is a lot to think about. But all these factors fit into one cohesive whole. We can look at Alan's story and follow his development as a way to see these points all fitting together more clearly.

Alan was born in a semi-rural, midwestern town, the youngest of three children and the only boy. He grew up with a traditional family structure, but his parents had a stormy relationship. The parents apparently tried to reconcile their differences for many years, but never managed to sustain a mutually supportive relationship. The father withdrew and only went through the motions of family life. He was either busy at work, reading about work at home, or away at the local bar. The mother showed her disappointment quite clearly, not hiding the fact that she always wanted more from her husband.

Alan's mother relied on her own mother for emotional support in raising her three children. However, financial support came from her husband, who continued in the role as provider, though it was obvious that there was little real relationship between the parents and only a superficial relationship between the father and his children.

Alan's mother constantly complained about her lot. Her first complaint was that she never had enough money, though she never tried to remedy the situation by working outside the home. Her husband was always the enemy, an easy target to blame for just about anything, simply because he was a man. She considered him responsible for whatever degree of happiness or unhappiness she had in life. She felt close to her mother and wanted the same kind of close ties to her daughters. What she wanted with her son, Alan, though, was different.

In Alan's mother's view, men held all the real power. (That is why her husband's failure took on such meaning.) Thus, in her mind, Alan had special power. She was captivated by him, admired him, and coddled him. She wanted him to go out into the world and be all he could be, all that she had expected her husband to be, and all that she herself felt she could not be. She wanted him to have all the advantages. When he asked for something, she thought he should have it. It seemed he could do no wrong.

Alan's sisters, of course, resented him. But they too thought men were more important than women. They could not complain directly about things they might have felt were unfair. But they did want extra attention from Alan, because he was male and important, and each thought that if she were deserving enough, he might treat her as special. Alan grew to feel that his mother and his sisters always wanted something from him, but he was never sure exactly what it was. He was special and "powerful," but he did not know why.

Alan's mother was angry at men in general, at her husband in particular, and at the second-rate position of women. But she never expressed this directly, except in complaints about her husband. And she did not use Alan as a whipping boy. She did not criticize or devalue him. Instead, she pushed him to achieve what she could not. This added to his feeling of being wonderful and entitled to the best.

The favored status that Alan held in his family is typical of the status of boys in many families. It mirrors the status of men in society in general. As noted earlier, men are the dominant group in our culture. As such, they are accorded power, recognition, and privilege. This status is reflected in family roles: often the girls are expected to do household chores, including the boys' laundry, while the boys pursue loftier pursuits, such as varsity sports. Or the boys are sent to the college of their choice, while the girls are expected to prepare themselves for marriage, no matter what the actual abilities and interests of the individual children may be.

In Alan's case, his mother, and her mother before her, lived with these values. This was the source of a great deal of the resentment and anger that Alan's mother felt in regard to his father. She believed he had all the rights and power; if her life was not going well, it was because he had not adequately used his power in her behalf. She assumed that Alan had the same kind of power and unconsciously expected that he would be able to provide for her what her husband had not.

In reality, Alan was a nice-looking young man, a bit reserved but pleasant and well-liked. He was quite intelligent and had graduated from college and completed graduate school before beginning a career as an accountant. (His mother and sisters, naturally, always expected him to prepare their taxes.) But he was no Superman, able to leap tall buildings at a single bound.

Soon after he began his career, Alan married his first real love. Julie was self-motivated, career-oriented, and easy to get along with. When Alan began having difficulty at his work and had to change jobs several times, Julie pitched in. She never seemed to complain, and Alan felt he could depend on her. He felt he was a good husband: he went to work every day and worked hard, brought home all of his money, loved Julie, brought her presents on birthdays and holidays, was faithful to her, helped around the house, and always tried to please her. She had lots of wishes, hopes, and dreams, and he thought he ought to satisfy her needs by doing what she wished. He didn't really enjoy many of these things, however, and, without realizing it, slowly and gradually, he, like his father, became sullen and withdrawn.

Then Julie began suffering from severe anxiety attacks, almost had to be hospitalized, and got involved in psychotherapy. As she recovered, Alan found out a lot about Julie. He was shocked to learn that after twelve years of what he had supposed was a mutually agreeable arrangement, Julie was actually resentful about the burden she had carried.

Alan also learned a good deal about himself, much of it having to do with his relationships with the women in his early life, especially his mother. Alan was raised by a woman, his mother, and he experienced himself as clearly different from her (and also from his two older sisters and his grandmother). He was a boy, but his mother and sisters were girls. His father was so uninvolved with the family that Alan couldn't connect much with him. But neither did he have much in common with all these females. He liked to play sports and army, while his sisters played with jacks and dolls. He had no interest in cooking or other household things. He just didn't fit in. This left him with a kind of anxiety and uncertainty about himself that was without words, that was largely outside of his awareness, but that nevertheless later affected his whole experience of himself as a man and as a man with women.

Alan was raised with traditional values, he was expected and expected himself to be strong and to support a family. But he also expected to be highly valued and catered to. Since he was supposed to be intrinsically important, he didn't think he should be criticized. Most criticisms, then, he tended to brush off. The ones that stuck stung him very hard, because he had never expected any and really didn't think he deserved any.

Pleasing his mother remained extremely important to him, though this goal was difficult to achieve because of her underlying resentment about her lot in life. Alan transferred his need to please onto Julie. He continued to see his masculine role as making women feel good, and he thought he was pretty good at it.

But he never felt like a real man. He actually felt sort of small. He had no solid, confident sense inside that he was undeniably male. For most of his childhood, he was being not-female, but he wasn't sure that he was really being male. He thought his behavior was appropriately masculine, but he thought that if anyone looked inside him, they would see how unsure of his masculinity he was. He was always hoping that he would catch up to the other guys and that no one would notice his inadequacy.

ALONE TOO SOON

Current theories of child development focus on the child's experience in its relationship with the caregivers in its life. (The framework described by Daniel Stern is most useful in understanding these early developments.)

At the beginning of life, the infant has a limited awareness of the caregiver, usually the mother, as a separate person. To the infant, its mother seems like an extension of itself, because she fixes what feels wrong to it. When the baby is hungry, it gets food; when it is wet, it gets dry; when it is lonely, it gets comforted. Initially, the infant does not have a distinct sense that it is another person who is doing the fixing. Things just get fixed.

Very soon, though, the infant gradually does become aware that this mother is an "other," and that the two of them are in a relationship. These are not thoughts, however; they are rudimentary awarenesses. This relationship is close, nurturing, comforting, and to the infant, it is everything—it is the whole world.

As the infant reaches the milepost of one year, his or her ability to make distinctions among people increases. As a part of this awareness, the infant begins to notice the differences between the sexes. The little boy is challenged by the discovery that he is not the same as his mother. The little girl, on the other hand, never feels this difference from her mother, because they are of the same gender. Before discovering the difference between himself and his mother, the boy could feel "Mother and I are one." And once he has experienced this difference between himself and his mother, he can never feel quite this way again. He is catapulted onto a path of separateness for which he is too young to be prepared psychologically. He will always feel different from Mother, and, in a sense, alone. Thus, though Alan was loved and cared for, he never could experience the profound warmth and solidarity of being *the same* as his mother.

Try to imagine a tiny, helpless person, just beginning to be aware of the world around him, permanently separated, psychologically, from his source of warmth and comfort. I think that it is difficult for us to imagine this, because we don't remember this kind of helplessness. But if we try, we can imagine the shock, fear, and confusion this toddler must feel. I think it feels as it would if you were all alone in a forest after dark and you didn't know whether or not anybody knew you were there. All of these feelings are pre-verbal—that is, since the child has not yet learned to speak, there are no words for them. But that nameless and powerful feeling that Alan and all men feel is all too real. It emphasizes a woman's importance, making her acceptance (even if she is in the other room, with no conversation) the basis of peace and joy. And it makes a woman's displeasure with a man terrible.

Because this trauma occurs before a child has words and before he has real thoughts, it is difficult to heal. If the little boy doesn't really know what is wrong, how can he get help? And if this trouble happens before he can think about it, how can he figure it out later, when he is bigger, stronger, and smarter? He can't, because he has nothing to remember, and so the trauma remains in its raw state. The boy moves through the rest of his life with a hidden loss and a hidden need. The need began as a need for mother, and it continues as a need for women.

In Alan, this showed up as a kind of anxious insecurity around women. He married Julie largely because of her confident manner. It made him feel safer. But he always had a feeling that something was not quite right within himself. Since he didn't know what this was, his strategy was to try to get away from the feeling in whatever ways he could. Julie felt this as a kind of avoidance that often left her feeling lonely when she was with Alan.

We now come to a bit of a twist in the story, a contradiction that develops out of what it is like to grow up as a boy, and specifically, what it is like to grow up as a boy in a patriarchal culture—a culture that values males more than females. Boys and girls are treated differently as they are being raised. From infancy on, girls are held and cuddled and talked to more than are boys. Boys are seen as needing less closeness and are talked to less and handled less.

In general, boys begin to develop their motor skills earlier than do girls. And so as they enter their toddler and childhood years, they are often too busy running and jumping to get much cuddling. Beyond this and other biological differences, however, are the social differences. We expect girls to be gentle and sweet-smelling, and even nurturing, and we expect boys to be adventurous, strong, and even naughty. They aren't expected to behave as well as girls are. But they are also supposed to be tough little soldiers. Big boys, after all, don't cry—and even little ones shouldn't.

So boys absorb the cultural messages and learn to be strong, tough, and brave. They learn that they may be allowed to get into a little bit of trouble, but that ultimately, they must toe the line. They learn that they will be expected to go to work, to provide for a family, and to go to war if necessary. At the very least, they learn that they should not show their feelings; better yet, they should not have feelings.

But here's the twist. In our culture, boys also learn a sense of entitlement. After all, men are the important people in the world. (Remember how Alan was raised.) Because of this status, they learn that they are important. All we have to do is look around us, and especially on TV and in newspapers and magazines, to know that the most "important" people are men. Boys may say that they want to be a fireman or a policeman when they grow up. They also say that they want to be President of the United States. They very often learn that they *should* get the things that they want, and very often from women.

We as women need to recognize our participation in this as we try to understand why men react to us in the ways that they do. We are, like it or not, a part of the culture that elevates men and devalues women. We absorb our cultural roles as well as do men. After all, we are the ones who lead men to believe that shirts appear, as if by magic, cleaned, pressed, and in their drawers! By living up to our role as helpers, nurturers, as the ones who meet men's ordinary daily needs, we cripple them in a sense. We handle them so quickly they don't even know they have these needs.

A confusing combination results. Men have a lot to live up to, as they have huge responsibilities in the outside world. Yet in their relationships, the responsibility to be responsive to the other person has been lifted from them. On the one hand, they are big, strong soldiers, providers for all; and on the other hand, they are helpless little boys who can't find a clean pair of socks.

In Alan, this difficulty showed up most clearly in his

relationship with Julie. Alan thought of himself as a responsible man. He had a solid job in a responsible profession, with a savings plan through his employer. He had served in the military for three years. From this he had gained confidence about his strength under pressure, and he still felt close ties to his buddies from his days of service. He thought that he was very responsibly meeting his obligations as a man and as a husband.

But to Julie, there were quite a few important things that she did for the two of them which Alan seemed never to help with and which he never seemed to notice or value. Alan thought he was quite enlightened; he even felt he was something of a feminist. He often prepared dinner when he arrived home from work before Julie. However, Julie prepared the shopping list and planned the meals. (And as Julie would point out, when Alan prepared dinner, it was usually hot dogs or tuna fish sandwiches.) She did the grocery shopping. She did their laundry, although Alan thought that, since he took his shirts to the cleaners, Julie wasn't doing *his* laundry. Julie actually planned the family's finances, paid the monthly bills, arranged vacations, and was the contact person for all their social plans. Because he had been catered to as a boy, Alan had never learned to do any of these things for himself. In fact, because of the lubrication Julie applied to his life, they were invisible to Alan. Somehow, they just happened. (Who wonders how gravity happens, or if it will stop?)

This lack of awareness in men is a result of the socialization process. In our society, as in most societies, males and females are expected to fulfill different roles. In fulfilling our cultural roles, we get a lopsided view of the world, of ourselves, and of others. We learn to value the norms that go along with our social role and to devalue those that are outside of that role, as well as the people for whom these are norms. A sense of security results from behaving as our roles dictate. We know what we are supposed to do, and we know who will approve of us. To break out of that role causes anxiety and discomfort.

Julie wants Alan to pay more attention to what goes on around him, to what goes into making a home comfortable. But he was never taught that. That's what girls are taught. And, of course, he certainly wouldn't want to do those things—they are girls' things. He must be different from a girl, because that is what it means to be a boy.

If we think back again to what childhood is like for a little boy, we see that he is raised primarily by someone who is not like he is. At first he has to deal with the loss of oneness with Mother. But then a bigger problem arises. The boy has to learn to be different from Mother. But since there isn't anything to be instead (since Father is not yet very clear to him) his only option is to be not-Mother. He has to try to be different than she is in all the ways that he can be. That is how he can be sure that he is a boy.

This goes on throughout life. Boys, and later men, actively reject any part of themselves that seems like a girl or a woman. For us, looking at this from the outside, it seems like needless posturing; after all, *we* are not in doubt that they are men. But *they* are. If we look at it from the inside (remember what we learned about blowing your nose in China), we see that the little boy discovers that he is a male, and not like Mother. After that awareness, he has to be not-Mother all the time *in order to be himself.*

What could be more important? Nothing is as important to human beings as having a good self-concept. We feel good when we feel sure of ourselves. For a man, then, a key part of feeling good about himself is to feel sure that he is a man. To do this, he has to be sure that he is not a woman.

LITTLE BOYS AND BIG MOTHERS

I know that I keep asking you to look at this again from another angle. And yes, I am asking you to do it again! This time, we'll look at the power of the mother.

Mother is the source of everything, for the little girl as well as for the little boy. But the girl has an advantage. She is like Mother, and she does not need to define herself as different from Mother. She becomes aware that she will be the same as Mother. Because of this, she does not experience the same kind of separation from Mother that the boy does. In fact, because of their alikeness, the girl has a sense of her mother's being inside her. This provides an important kind of security. The all-giving person is a person just like her, and so, not so far away from her. Even if we women have conflicts with our mothers, we still have a wordless sense of continuity within ourselves because of our sameness.

For the boy, however, the source of everything is outside of himself. This big mother has the power to give or to withhold, the power to make the world a safe, secure place, or the dark forest in which he is lost and alone. The boy, and later the man, experiences all women as possessing this power.

This kind of early relationship between the boy and his mother affects later relationships between men and women in general. Women are a source of great comfort and satisfaction, and also a source of great danger. Men develop psychological defenses to cope with this frightening feeling. The whole culture, too, reacts to this difficulty. Men are supposed to be the strong ones, yet they feel vulnerable to women. A belief system has developed to hide this paradoxical condition. We will look at this in more detail at the end of this chapter. But first, let us look at one more important factor in the little boy's childhood.

DADDY, WHERE ARE YOU?

Although things are now changing in many families, and we may see further shifts in future generations, fathers have been largely absent in the lives of little boys. The most tragic example of this is seen in inner-city ghetto life, in which it is sadly common for families to have no father at all. Boys raised in this environment have a terrible time making their way in the world. And their behavior is often an exaggeration of stereotypic masculine traits. That is all they have to go on. The lure of gangs is understandable in this context. Even in less extreme circumstances, the relative lack of Father still has a profound effect on the boy's developing identity as a male. Without a clear experience of Father in his everyday life, learning to be a boy is very difficult.

As Alan's parents struggled with their difficulties, Alan's father became less and less involved in family life. Even though not all families have such overt difficulties, the withdrawal of Father from activities at home is quite common. Fathers traditionally have not been a central part of child-rearing. They may love their children and feel committed to their families, but they feel that they show their love by providing for the family. Their time and attention have usually been focused elsewhere: on work.

Fathers work. That is the way it is. This is a very deeply ingrained cultural belief. Men who choose a nontraditional lifestyle are not approved of by other men. And women who are more successful than their husbands usually have difficulty with that kind of role. Most men believe that to be a good husband and father means to provide a good salary. So this means that the father will be away from the family most of the time, doing what he is supposed to do.

This causes the most trouble for the little boy. He has just discovered that he is not a female. He has to learn to be different from his mother. He is supposed to be like his father. But his father isn't there. His father is off somewhere else, acting masculine. What the boy has most information about is concrete or superficial things about his father. He can carry tools around in his pocket, he can watch television, or he can mimic his father's expressions.

But he has little time to be with his father and feel what he is like. All he can do is try to copy his actions.

The boy can learn to go to work, to fix things, to always have something important to do. In very traditional families, he may also learn to give orders and to expect to be catered to. He will probably learn to be interested in sports. But it is unlikely that he will learn to *feel* what it is like to be a man. What he does learn is that to feel like a man is to *not feel.*

The father is not only physically distant, but also emotionally distant. The boy cannot have the same kind of close emotional bond with him that he initially had with his mother. Don't forget, the boy has to be more distant from his mother in order to have his own identity as a boy. But there is no male person with whom he can have that closeness instead. Without this natural connection, it is difficult for the boy to have a sense of himself as a male that is comfortable and secure. His sense of himself as a man is something that he must create and depends on his *actions* (doing masculine things) rather than on his *feelings.*

Because his masculine identity is based on what he does, it is never secure. It isn't permanent, but it has to be recreated and reasserted over and over again. It is through action that his masculinity is verified. For a man, to *be* is to *do.*

As a result of this series of struggles in development, the boy's masculine identity rarely gets truly solidified. It remains tenuous throughout life. This often results in exaggerated or stereotyped masculine behaviors—a man doesn't feel like a man unless he acts like one.

I'M NOT A WOMAN, BUT WHAT IS A MAN?

For Alan, his father's emotional distance was the greatest problem. His father was distant from the entire family. His sisters could get a sense of their femininity from their mother, but Alan was left out in the cold. He never felt that he was quite "doing it right" as a man. That is why his army experience, with its memories of feeling that he was doing what men do, with men, in a man's world, remained so important to him. But when he was with Julie, he was never really sure about himself as a man. His insecurity led him to retreat. He would become distant or get involved in his own projects. This served two purposes. His absorption in his own projects could block out the anxiety. And being active, as well as emotionally distant, as his father was, were the only things he did know about how to be a man.

COPING STRATEGIES, DEFENSIVE MANEUVERS

Women have always been a powerful force in the world. Men are vulnerable to us. But this is not talked about openly; it is not an agreed-upon part of common knowledge. It is like the story of the emperor's new clothes. No one seems willing to acknowledge this truth. I believe that there are two main reasons for this, both centering around men's vulnerability.

The first is men's need to protect themselves. Why should they acknowledge this reality? The currently accepted reality (like the reality that the emperor is wearing beautiful clothes) supports their power. It would not be safe for men to examine and acknowledge their neediness for women, their dependency. No, men are strong and powerful, more important, more intelligent, and more valuable than women. Period. Their very vulnerability leads them to act and think as if they were invulnerable.

The second reason is women's role of protecting men. In the culture at large, we perpetuate the belief that men are the important ones. In our relationships with them, we protect their self-images by fostering this belief. In private, we talk about how inadequate they are (remember the joke that "Women often have to do the work of two men in half the time. . . . Luckily, this is not difficult"), while in public, we protect them from feeling or appearing weak.

Since I am writing about men, I will focus on men's defensive strategies. But in terms of understanding our cultural system and how it works, it helps to think about our own, too. For we are part of the system of pumping up men at the expense of ourselves.

We all experienced the power of a woman when we were infants. We all were most dependent on her when we were in our most helpless state. Because it originates in infancy, the helplessness we feel in relation to a woman is at a deeper, more primitive, and wordless level than helplessness in relation to a man.*

Now, this is true for both males and females. However,

---

*See Dorothy Dinnerstein: *The Mermaid and the Minotaur* for more on this idea.

the situation is more dangerous for men than for women because of their additional need to distance themselves from women in order to feel clearer about themselves as men. This has resulted in traditions that are found in every culture that keeps women down, and therefore make women less dangerous. The sense of fear of the powerful natural force of women gets controlled in many ways: women may be segregated, confined, or avoided. (Think of all the religions in which women are separated from and have less power than men.) Our culture has institutionalized many actions that come out of this need to put women down, such as the earlier inability to vote or the readiness with which we comment on a woman's beauty rather than her intelligence or power.

I am here reminded of the expectation that men will spend two months' salary to buy the appropriate diamond engagement ring for a fiancée. Yes, this is a burden (although it is also a way of saying, "Look at how successful I am"). Further, it can act as a piece of distancing from women. It may be a kind of gift-giving that is distanced from emotion, another form of doing rather than feeling. If a man treats a woman like a princess, and feels like this is his obligation as well as something that she demands in order to be appeased, he does not have to experience his own deep feelings: the fear of commitment to another person, the hopes attached to such a relationship, and the real dependence on this other person for his future happiness.*

*See *Why Men Are the Way They Are* for more on this idea.

Alan had this kind of dependence on Julie. But his defenses worked so well that he was literally unaware of this feeling. Although he was aware that in many concrete ways Julie was "dependable," he didn't feel his *emotional* dependence on her. His denial of this dependency became a difficulty for Julie. No matter how much she did, she never felt from Alan that he was actually grateful to her. Also, as many women do, Julie felt that her kind of care-giving (emotional support and attention to the details and aesthetics of daily living) should be mutual, and that when Alan could, he would return the effort. But he never did. From his perspective, he was doing more than enough. Why would he think differently?

Alan, too, had a double dose of this dependency problem. Not only did he need to defend himself generally against the importance of women because of being a male raised by a female. But Alan's mother herself was a difficult person to get along with. She was always complaining, and the cause for her complaints was usually Alan's father. That gave Alan another reason to be wary of Julie's importance to him and to keep his distance from her when he felt his vulnerability to her; if he did not, he might feel as if he were his father, constantly criticized by his mother.

OTHER WOMEN

A part of Alan was afraid that all women would be like his mother, never satisfied. He therefore saw Julie's complaints as if they were his mother's, constant and pointless.

Julie was trying to be as polite and unprovocative as she could. But Alan was not likely to see it that way. In addition, Alan's mother's style of complaining was annoying, and Alan defended against that, too. With Julie, this showed up as a kind of automatic tuning her out, just in case what she said would be unpleasant.

This last aspect of Alan's distancing from Julie is something that happens to all of us in important relationships. When a person does something that is in any way similar to a past important relationship, it triggers old feelings from the past and the old automatic ways of handling them. We then respond to the new person as if he or she were the old person and we had to take the same old (invisible, automatic) actions.

For a man, his relationship with his actual mother, with all her personality characteristics, and all the circumstances of their life together will mold how he sees, feels, and experiences, and reacts to women. This will influence his relationships with the other important women in his life. In Alan's case, Julie came to represent the parts of his mother that he wanted to get away from.

In her therapy with Alan, Julie had some hard work ahead of her. She might tell Alan that she wasn't just complaining, but Alan wasn't likely to hear it. If she explained what she needed and gave legitimate reasons, Alan tended to automatically discount the validity of what she said as she said it as he had learned to do with his mother. When Julie told him of her pain, he shied away from acknowledging that he had any responsibility for it when in fact he already felt guilty and inadequate. Because of this guilt, he did not really listen to her complaints about his contribution to her problems.

An important part of the work in this kind of therapy is for both people to understand together what Alan's problems were with his mother and then to clarify the ways in which Julie was different from Alan's mother. It is difficult work, because Alan's automatic, unconscious emotional response to Julie is really a reaction to his mother. And because it is automatic and habitual, it takes a long time to change.

There is another important reason why this is difficult to change. Remember, the woman is the center of everything. The man must please her in order to feel secure that she will stay with him. (Unfortunately, he often doesn't feel that he is loved for himself, but rather for what he can do.) If Alan admits how much he has hurt Julie, he also has to realize that he has already jeopardized the relationship through his actions. Ironic as it is, the more insecure Alan is with the relationship with Julie, the harder it will be to do what will make the relationship more secure!

Sometimes it is relationships with other important women that are an important cause of the problem. Often, this will be a relationship with an ex-wife or an ex-girlfriend. The man may react to the person with whom he is currently involved as if he were in the past. Sometimes this is hard to understand. After all, if that relationship was painful, isn't he glad to be in a different one? Why would he want to re-live it? The reason is that he is doing what he learned to do, and he will continue to do it until he learns something new.

SUMMING UP

Women scare men to death. Like it or not, we have to face this if we really want to understand them better. Even though we feel like little girls, needing a daddy, even though we feel discounted and devalued, even though we feel powerless, we appear otherwise to men. To men, we have all the power. We have the wordless power, frightening because it is so primitive, that comes from that early time in life when there is only need and satisfaction of that need. Since we are female, we still represent the satisfaction of that need.

It is frightening to feel totally vulnerable to another person. It is this vulnerability that men feel with us. And it is this vulnerability that men protect themselves from by being distant, hostile, preoccupied, devaluing, and sexualizing. Anything they can do to feel as if they are not subject to us protects them from these vulnerable feelings.

All of us need to have a clear, solid sense of ourselves. Because of the relative closeness to Mother, and the relative distance from Father, and because they have to disidentify with Mother (that is, learn to be not like her), men have a tenuous sense of themselves and their masculinity. They have to assert over and over again that, yes, they are real men.

In succeeding chapters, we will see many ways in which these issues show up in the lives of men and in men's relationships with women.

Chapter Three

STRUCTURE

Roy ends every weekend with his Sunday evening ritual. He likes to wash and vacuum his car, and he also likes to get the garage swept out. He likes to start the week this way, because, although he doesn't even admit it to himself, he feels a little bit nervous about going back into the office on Monday mornings.

First he wipes down and vacuums the inside of the car. Then he washes and dries the outside. (He does all this at the local car wash if it's too cold to do it at home.) Then he sweeps out the garage and makes sure all the tools are in their places. Finally, he parks his clean car in his clean garage and goes inside, tired, but relaxed and satisfied.

Louise would like, every now and then, to go to a movie on Sunday evening, or to go out for dinner. But she can't get Roy to join her, because it makes him nervous to alter his routine. In fact, once a month he adds the sorting and filing of the family bills and receipts. It's a hopeless battle for Louise. Roy is in his own private world on Sunday afternoons. He won't tamper with a routine that works.

*   *   *

Josh is a corporate executive with a hefty six-figure income. He lives in a large house on a large piece of property, but he still mows his own lawn. He never thinks it's done well enough when somebody else does it. When he has the edges all neat and crisp, then all is in order, and Josh feels good. He is always firing landscaping services so he can do the lawn himself. After a tense week at the office, an afternoon of mowing and edging is just the cure he needs. All the stresses of the office melt away. All the conflicts between colleagues, all the pressure he feels to continue to excel, all the worries about how fast his money is going recede into the distance as the even regularity of the freshly cut lawn emerges from under his mower.

Roy and Josh are keeping things in order for the purpose of handling their feelings or anxieties. But there is an internal kind of ordering that men do that, though often invisible, is even more common and profound.

Shirley and Ron are finishing a romantic dinner at a beachside restaurant. The last colors of the sunset are just leaving the sky.

Shirley is feeling full of warmth and emotion and wants to be close to Ron. She asks him what he is feeling.

He says, "Please, don't ask."

She says, "But I really want to know what you have on your mind."

"No, you don't; trust me," he pleads.

"Yes, I do, I really do. Please tell me."

"All right," he says, after continued coaxing. "I was thinking, 'I wonder what would have happened if Montana had passed long instead of short on that key third down at the end of the third quarter.' "

I love this story. It captures a common experience. But though I first heard it told by a comedian, it's no joke. That man really was thinking about the San Francisco Forty-Niners, while the woman was thinking about how much she liked him and hoped that their relationship continued to grow. He wasn't paying attention to how he was feeling. He was there, with her, but disconnected at a potentially emotional, sentimental time. He was calculating, analyzing, keeping score—in order to handle his feelings in the situation.

How is this possible? How could he be so out of touch with the emotions in this setting? Easy. This is the natural state of affairs for men. In this chapter I will explain what this state is, why it occurs, and how we as women can understand it, adapt to it, and, from time to time, modify it.

KEEPING THINGS IN ORDER

"Structure" is the term that I will be using to describe what men do and think that puts things in order, that regulates, that organizes, that enumerates, that fits things into rules and patterns, and that functions to limit and contain emotions. Men do these things almost all the time. Sometimes their behavior in this regard is invisible, as it would have been in the last example if Shirley hadn't asked what Ron was thinking. Or the behavior might be more apparent, like Roy's need to have a clean car every Monday morning. But even when we see obvious behavior, such as Roy's, we don't know much about the purpose it serves, or about how important it is.

Some everyday examples of structure include such things as making sure that the records and CD's are in alphabetical order or timing how long it takes to ride two miles on the exercise bike each day. Men are always organizing and counting this way. It is such a common stance for men that I would venture to say that, if a man says or does something or reacts in a way that you don't understand, you'll be able to figure it out pretty quickly if you think of the "structure."

This is such a basic part of men's psychological make-up that it is operating virtually all of the time. And, like anything else, it has its pros and its cons. We may complain about it and make jokes about it, but ultimately we rely on it because the ability to structure is what enables a person to keep his cool in a crisis. Men are raised to do this, and they tend to be pretty good at it. Unfortunately, the same skill is "in use" most of the time, including when men are spending non-crisis time with women.

That's the part that we don't understand and that bothers us. We don't tend to complain when a man takes care of business efficiently, when he changes the tire when we're out in the country and it's raining, or when he's able to put everything we want to bring on a trip into the trunk, including the beach chairs we thought there wasn't room for. But we don't like it when the same stance makes him unaware of us on an emotional or feeling level. That's when we are distressed.

Women complain that men don't show their feelings, that they seem like robots, that there's no expression on their faces. In an emergency, though, when a woman may be crying or expressing fear, a man who shows no emotion may be setting out a plan for handling things and directing people to do what needs to be done.

Why do men structure things all the time? Why does everything have to be organized, enumerated, and calculated? Why can't things just be? Much of the explanation comes from what has been discussed in chapters 1 and 2: first, that men are soldiers, and so they march to orders, and expect things to operate according to standard rules; and second, that men have to deal with the anxiety of a premature separation from and loss of Mother. Because of this loss, they need something reassuring to take the place of that connection. And whatever that something is, it will be important, central, and strong.

Of course, socialization is an important part of how men learn to structure. Men are trained to behave in certain ways, and they learn to copy other men—who are usually focusing on order, regulation, and numbers. If a boy is copying his father, for example, he probably will be trying to look like someone who gets the job done and who does not show any expression on his face; if he's copying an older, "cooler" friend, he will be doing the same.

But it is the issue of the early separation from Mother that has the most profound psychological consequences and that sets this structuring process in motion. We will focus on this aspect, because it helps explain the part of structuring that is hardest for us to see—the internal part, the way a man is *inside*.

MEN'S LOST SECURITY

My husband explains the issue of security to me frequently. "You are lucky that you are a woman," he says. "You have your mother inside of you. There's a way that you don't have to worry about how you are going to feel safe by making your connection with her. It's with you all the time."

He says that he has to make up for not having that, and that it takes work. And the world never seems to feel as safe to him. I guess I believe him, although what he describes is so different from my own experience that it is difficult to understand and to accept.

But the explanation makes sense. The structure shows up most clearly at the times of the greatest stress. When a man is threatened, that's when the fewest feelings show. Instead, he devises a plan or a procedure to follow. That is what to look for when you're trying to see how structure serves a protective function.

"Star Trek" is full of examples of men using structure. Think of Captain Kirk, sitting at the controls on the bridge, being told that the "Shields are not operating" and that the approaching enemy has destroyed "the last eight Starfleet ships it has encountered." There sits Kirk, saying, "Stay on course. Go to warp speed." You can't see what he is feeling. There is no expression on his face. In fact, he isn't really feeling anything at all. But you know that he is coming up with a plan. And of course there is Mr. Spock. He is the essence of structure! He doesn't even know what a feeling is. (And he's not supposed to be human. And funny, so many men want to be just like him!)

And I think of Henry and Sue. They were seeing me for marital problems, and in the course of this therapy, Henry had finally become aware of his feelings and was seriously considering continuing on in his own psychotherapy. Then their daughter, Lisa, was in a serious auto accident. She had serious fractures to her legs and hips that would require multiple surgeries to repair. It was doubtful that she would ever function normally again, though it was hoped that she would be able to walk.

The accident disrupted marital therapy for a time, though Henry and Sue rose to the occasion and were able to handle many difficulties better than they had in the past. In the face of their crisis, they realized that they had a lot to be thankful for, and that they wanted to stop being so critical of each other. Instead, they wanted to work together to make the adjustments in their family life that would be required by Lisa's long illness and recovery.

Sue wanted to continue meeting with me in order to work on her personal issues. If there ever was a time when she needed help, this was it. She cried in our sessions and talked about how overwhelmed she felt. Henry, on the other hand, was ready to stop. He had put the marital problems on the back burner. He was worried about the new medical expenses, and he felt the marriage was stable enough to handle the crisis. He wasn't thinking about the feelings that had been bothering him anymore. But mostly, I think that he didn't want the therapy to force him to acknowledge the feelings he had about Lisa. It would have been too disruptive to him. Of course he didn't say that, or even recognize it. He wouldn't be able to keep on top of his situation if he felt his anxiety. He was going to take charge and organize things, and being in touch with his feelings was no way to accomplish that!

Henry responded to extreme stress by getting organized. He structured life for the crisis around Lisa, and his feelings were regulated, even gone. And Captain Kirk surely has reason to go into an emergency mode, with his ship always being under attack. So does Henry. And although these examples are rather extreme, men are working in this "structure" almost all the time. Do they feel so much danger *all* of the time that they have to respond as if they were? After all, *their* ship isn't about to be destroyed.

In fact, men do feel in danger, but the danger that men feel, which is usually invisible to us, is the danger that began in infancy. It is the loss of safety that comes with the loss of Mother. Remember that the little boy loses her too early. What he is left with is the distance between them, but he has nothing with which to replace her. He cannot look to his father as a substitute; fathers generally don't do the same kind of nurturing. They are not consistently present, as is Mother. They are generally not as soothing and gentle. Fathers teach their children about the world at large—they may play with them, but they rarely get to know them as people. And of course they often are not even around enough, as they are focused on work or other activities.

The little boy moves into a void, away from the giver of everything. When I think of this, it begins to remind me of what it might feel like to be out in space with my ship about to be destroyed. This is an intolerable condition for a child. Research shows that infants deprived of mothering get very depressed, stop thriving, and even die.

The void is death itself. Something must replace it. And for men, what replaces it is structure. In the absence of the *concrete, secure* presence of Mother, something else that is concrete and secure, dependable and substantial must take her place to protect the boy from the terror of abandonment and from fear. Structure replaces the lost connection with Mother, and it is as important to a man as Mother was.

The psychological vulnerability caused by the early separation from Mother is a constant internal state of affairs. It does not, therefore, have much to do with external circumstances. Thus, ordinary daily life requires the use of the structure. It is not used only for unmistakable emergencies; we see it in operation all the time. When you ask a man what should be done for someone who's upset, he's likely to say, "So, she's upset. She'll get over it." Then he's finished with the problem; he doesn't have to let it disrupt him anymore. Or if dinner gets ruined just before the guests arrive, he may say, "Don't worry. We'll find something to give them. They won't care." He has an answer to the problem, and that means that there is no longer anything to feel. And then there is the painfully familiar response to the question "How are you feeling?" The answer so often seems to be a brief and unsatisfying "Fine."

What we see in these everyday examples is the insulation that the structure provides. A man is protected from feelings of all kinds, all of the time. And, while he is insensitive to other people's feelings, he is also insensitive to his own.

This concept helped me finally understand what had been bothering me in my relationship with my father for years and years. Now, my father is not a cold, insensitive man. He is a college professor and is much beloved by his students. My problem with him was that whenever I was embarking on a new venture that presented risk as well as opportunity, all he seemed to focus on was the risk. He never seemed to get enthusiastic or excited for me. He immediately began pointing out the hazards and the pitfalls. (As though I hadn't thought of any of these things myself.) I was left with the feeling that he would always put a damper on everything. When I finally managed to confront him about this, he acted surprised, but then understood what I meant. He told me, "I was only saying to you the same things I would say to myself." It finally made sense. If he wouldn't let himself get carried away by his own feelings, why would he get carried away with mine?

Structure is all around; it takes many forms and functions at many different times. It is a protector. It is also a screen, a barrier, that can keep potentially hurtful things out. This barrier or screen is like a grid that organizes reality. It is the way the little boy learned to handle his world, and therefore it is the pattern through which he now views the world. It allows the boy to look at the world one step removed, because everything that comes at him is filtered by this screen, this grid, this organizing principle.

As good as his grid is at providing safety, it is equally bad at discriminating. Traumatic and painful feelings can be filtered out as they come through the screen. However, *all* other kinds of feelings are filtered out as well. So even clearly pleasurable feelings, such as those associated with getting a raise, or acing a serve in tennis, are not always fully experienced. The defense mechanism in this pattern brings with it a general muting of feelings, a kind of psychic numbing. This is the predominant means available to men for handling their feelings. So if men let down this screen in order to let feelings in, they are left literally defenseless.

When Beth and Arnie talk about their problems in therapy, Beth is quite expressive and Arnie is quite reserved, looking at the world through his screen. Beth pleads with Arnie to share his feelings with her. When he finally lets down his guard, she feels he is finally with her, listening. But she is angry with him, and she takes this opportunity to tell him about how hurt and angry she is because of his behavior. Arnie is speechless. His face is expressionless. He knows how to keep the impact of Beth's feelings out. If he lets them in, he will have no skills with which to deal with them. He is defenseless, once he has let down his grid. What Beth interprets as not caring, not feeling, is really the face of a man with nowhere to go, no way to think, floating in a void.

You've seen this before, and you probably think it means that a man doesn't care, doesn't feel. But that is not the case. What it means is terror and helplessness, often covered over as quickly as possible with anger. If you watch a man's reaction from this perspective, you will see it. And you then may see that the anger that often accompanies the screen is a protection from the helplessness and fear.

The structure, the protector, is all around. It is a dependable support, an ally for helping to handle painful feelings. It is security, the substitute for Mother, the replacement for the warm, secure feeling from which the boy was cut off too soon. It provides a sense of safety in the world. Just about the only time a man is without it is when he is taking the risk of allowing himself to be close to a woman.

Most men are unaware of this defensive pattern, in the same way that we are all oblivious to our habitual defensive patterns. Men are not likely to describe their behavior as "structure" because they are not aware of it as such. They can probably describe some of their behaviors that serve to structure, such as counting, measuring, being logical and organized, being in control of their feelings. But because they are unaware of this behavior as a pattern and as a defense, they are unaware that it is not all of reality. So, naturally, they are unaware of how their behavior would affect someone else who lives in a different reality. They are unaware of how this behavior affects women.

Men can relate to each other quite well through the structure. It is comfortable and familiar to them. It actually gives them a common language and experience through which to communicate. It's one reason that men so much enjoy reminiscing with each other about their army days. Everything is understood between them; nothing has to be explained. The feelings that are painful will, by common understanding, be protected against. Their war stories will be funny, while the war itself and their overall experiences were not.

Within the framework provided by structure, men can express a huge number of ideas, concerns, even worries and fears. But these emotions are not expressed as such. The structure puts them in code. They come out as plans, outlines, solutions, or as the deliberate and understood absence of an issue or feeling. They are outlined and limited by the structure, which keeps men safe from uncontrolled emotions.

This is exactly what Henry did when his daughter was injured. He put himself on a schedule and tried to keep everyone else on schedule, too. He talked to the physical therapist every Monday and Friday morning; he set aside time to work with Lisa on her exercises every evening. He took over paying the bills so that he could see each medical bill as it came in and make sure that it got paid on time. There simply wasn't room for feelings.

THE COMFORT IN RULES

Structure provides the kind of soothing and protecting that a mother would do if she were there to soothe the boy. That is a lot of very important comforting and soothing. Structure is there instead of a person, doing what a person would do. A man will, understandably, be very attached to it, related to it, and dependent on it, as a child would be with a parent. He is dependent on it as any of us would be on someone or something that takes care of us. The structure contains and handles the kind of feelings that a little boy might have, that are still there when he is grown, when he has to handle them "like a man."

There is safety in order. It is reassuring to men to know just how things will be done and to then have some ability to predict how they will turn out. If you think about things in a routine way, then they seem more predictable. If things are predictable, then you can believe that you can have some control over things. Having a sense of control, after all, makes a lot of people feel safe. Order, then, is a kind of structure. The routine way of doing things, the predictability, may look simply like lack of spontaneity, a robotlike way of behaving. But it feels comfortable and safe. And in its own way it actually feels *good*.

This is why it is so important to Roy that the car be washed and the garage swept and straightened every Sunday. It's predictable and dependable. Similarly, Josh feels safe when the lawn is edged. Everything is where it should be.

Numbers are a very important part of structure, too. (In fact, they are so important that I've included a whole chapter on the meaning and importance of numbers in the lives of men.) When things can be counted, they again seem to be under more control. The unpredictable becomes predictable when it can be counted, tabulated, and made into statistics. The numbers themselves then form a whole reality that can be manipulated and understood. Numbers are another way that men can handle situations, including those involving feelings, that may otherwise seem out of control. Safe again!

Safety, predictability, comfort through order and control, and reassurance are the recurring themes of structure. The outward appearance may be rigidity, compulsivity, preoccupation with numbers and information, and an appearance of emotionlessness.

As soothing, comfortable, and familiar as this structure is to men, it is only the outward appearance of it that is visible to women. Therefore, women don't, in general, really know about this aspect of men. We don't think about the meaning of it; we only know what it looks like.

In *Her Mother's Daughter*, Marilyn French describes how structure looks to a woman:

> What I did was act like a man. I blanked out all expression from my face and stuck my hand out to shake his. I hollowed out my voice, and acted a little cool and a little weary as if I had to make hundreds of trips like this. It helped that I was tired; I didn't have the energy to be expressive. He responded to this; ... and began to treat me professionally.

And again,

> ... my major problem is not men but the fact that I have become one of them, inexpressive and unable to feel, all tight inside like a sealed tank that threatens to explode if the safety valve is loosened.

The external aspect of the structure is relatively easy to see. It is more difficult to understand the important meanings of the behavior and the feelings and needs that underlie it. We as women feel cut off from men emotionally as they seem to value their structures more than they value being with us. We feel sad and lonely when men don't share themselves and their feelings with us the way we want to do with them. Understanding the meanings of the behavior helps us feel less rejected. We may be able to feel less hurt and angry, and that always makes it easier to find creative solutions.

I'm sure that it is irritating when I say again that this behavior that we dislike so much in men is the result of men's vulnerability. We're tired of feeling that we are always taking care of them, and we don't look forward to another version of that same message. But it is our awareness of the *causes* and *purposes* of this behavior that we can use to create change.

Let's go back to Arnie and Beth. If Beth wants to hear about what is important to Arnie, perhaps she could ask him how he would like to express this. Maybe it won't be the same way that she would express it, in terms of feelings. Maybe Arnie would prefer to write down his concerns, instead of voicing them face to face. Perhaps a list would be the most comfortable format for him. He might even prefer to rate them. That should be acceptable to Beth, at least for a start. There is no absolute value that says that Beth's way of expressing herself is so much better, although as women it is what we are more comfortable with.

Beth can learn to be aware of how threatening it is to Arnie to express his feelings. She can think about how exposed and defenseless it makes him feel. She might feel that way herself if she were not allowed to express her feelings. As it is, she feels relieved when she can express her feelings. For Arnie, though, expressing feelings is like entering a territory in which he has no knowledge, experience, or control. He feels stupid and clumsy as well as frightened, and he often just goes blank.

To get another view of what this is like for Arnie, imagine that Arnie told Beth that he really needed her to dismantle the engine of his car and then put it back together. And suppose he wanted her to do it now, or he'd feel so dissatisfied he might have to think of leaving the relationship. The degree of importance to Arnie wouldn't give Beth the first clue about how to take an engine apart and put it back together! But that is how Arnie feels when she challenges him to express himself without his familiar guard being up. He doesn't know how to do it. He has to learn. She can teach him if she thinks of him as being frightened, helpless, insecure, and a little embarrassed, instead of as cold and withholding.

If Louise wants to go to a movie on Sunday evening, perhaps she can encourage Roy to clean up the garage a little earlier in the afternoon, instead of trying to get him to give it up altogether. Maybe she could even help him in the interests of getting the job done faster. That way, Roy might not feel that his favorite routine is threatened. And when he is not under attack, he is safer, as we all are. Someday he might be able to relax.

We might not particularly like the compromises that we have to make in working some of these things out with men. But they are shackled to their defenses, because it feels to them as if their lives depend on them. Perhaps I shouldn't even call these structures defenses, because that can sound like something superficial, something tacked on, something that can be changed or gotten rid of. But the structure is *reality* for men, not something outside of them, but invisibly part of them. As infants, they weren't lucky enough to feel as secure as we did at the same age, so they have to create that security now. Helping them feel more secure may eventually make some of those defenses less necessary. And understanding why those "defenses" are there can make certain behaviors a lot easier to tolerate, and at times maybe even endearing.

Chapter Four

TRANCE

Ed is in heaven. In front of him, sitting in its own space in the entertainment center, is his new CD player. It has a five-disc changer and a 128-channel programmable remote. The new equipment sits next to the VCR and the television, right above the tuner and amplifier.

In his left hand is the new remote control for the CD player. In his right is the television remote control. He is flipping through channels on the TV as he programs his CD player to play only his favorite songs, skipping over the ones he doesn't like.

Nothing impinges on his reverie. He is content and at peace. The house could quite literally catch fire and he wouldn't notice. His world is contained in his entertainment equipment and his control over it; he has no thought for anything else.

Connie carries to the table for Christmas dinner the heaping plate of turkey that her husband Chuck has carved. Everyone sits, waiting, ready for the feast. (The kids are planning to eat very little turkey, having seen a chocolate pecan pie in the kitchen.) The ritual is wearing thin for Connie.

Great Aunt Norma has never been anyone's favorite relative. But there she sits, at her usual place at the head of the table. Everyone feels somewhat obligated to her. She has helped with Peter's college tuition, money for Suzanne's surgery, contacts that enabled Paul to get his job. But she is overbearing, loud, demanding, self-serving, and critical.

As Norma begins questioning the children about their school performances, Connie looks over at Chuck. He's already gone. Mechanically, he loads his plate with food and begins to eat calmly and methodically. He says nothing. He hardly ever looks up, and when he does, Connie sees no expression in his eyes. He is out of contact range. He might as well be on another planet.

Norma is his great aunt. It's because of his family obligations that she comes and turns every Christmas dinner from a friendly time to be together into an ordeal to be endured. And Chuck does nothing. He says nothing. Connie is suffering, but Chuck is so far away that he doesn't feel a thing.

Ann came to therapy to get help with depression. She had had a serious problem with alcohol abuse and had managed to quit drinking on her own. After she had been sober for several months, though, her underlying depression became apparent to her. Her awareness of her feelings unclouded by alcohol, she has begun to identify how lonely she is in her marriage to Tony.

A kind and gentle man, Tony is not very adept at being in an intimate relationship, committed though he is to his marriage and to Ann. When in doubt, which is, unfortunately, often, he tunes out. Physically present, he is emotionally absent. In these "tuned-out" states, he rarely shows much pleasure or sadness, he speaks in a monotone, and his face is usually blank.

When Ann first told me that she thought that Tony was "in a trance," the description was so apt that I wondered why we hadn't all been using it for years. For it clearly points to an experience that many women have of men. There are countless women who are in relationships with men who appear to be physically present but who are personally absent.

SELF-HYPNOTIC OBLIVION

The "trance" describes the very common appearance and behavior that many women see in the men with whom they are involved. Let me explain why I say "involved." This trance is a way that men frequently meet the world. It is a way of being that happens in all places and at any time. But we are most aware of it in the men with whom we have close relationships.

There are two main reasons for this. The first is that once a woman is involved with a man, she wants a deeper emotional connection. She is not satisfied with ordinary superficial communication. She wants to really *be* with him, and she therefore notices when he only *seems* to be with her but really isn't.

The second reason is that, for the man, an intense, intimate relationship is much more threatening than a casual one. Remember, we women have a great deal of power, and we threaten his vulnerability, whether we try to or not. So he has more need for his defenses when we are getting close to him. Since closeness is dangerous for a man, he must protect himself against it. And the trance is a defense that goes into action and protects him from the situation that seems to him to be the most dangerous.

We women love to talk. It's our best way of connecting with each other. Sometimes what we talk about is deeply important to us, and sometimes it's pretty trivial. But when we are talking with each other, we feel tuned in and involved.

It isn't the same for men. Talking demands a kind of continuous involvement that they usually avoid. There's too much connection and emotion involved, too much demand for constant responses. Men aren't very good at that. It threatens *their* sense of peace and security, which, for them, is provided by structure, by distance from feelings.

I am reminded of an old joke, about a man who goes to the doctor to get his hearing checked. After the exam, the doctor says to him, "Well, you're not doing too badly, but you are beginning to lose some of the hearing in your left ear."

The man goes home, and his wife asks him what the

doctor said. The man hesitates briefly, and then says, "He says you should talk into my left ear."

You can look at this story in two ways. One way is to think of it as making fun of the wife who talks too much. That's not what's funny to me. To me it makes fun of the man who needs to not hear, the man who needs to tune out, to be in a trance.

The men that we are talking about are often called absent-minded, irresponsible, even childlike. They seem oblivious to their present circumstances. These men are not actually deficient or lacking in competence, though they appear to be so. After all, the "absent-minded professor" is hardly stupid; it's just that he has "loftier" matters to consider and is too preoccupied to pay attention to day-to-day events in the world around him.

When men are in this state, they are in a kind of self-hypnosis, an efficient, self-soothing state in which most external influences are filtered out. Although we think of hypnosis as having to do with women, in fact, being in a trance is absolutely male.

Recently, I looked up "trance" in the dictionary. There were three definitions: "(1) a state of partly suspended animation or inability to function: stupor; (2) a somnolent state (as of deep hypnosis); (3) a state of profound abstraction or absorption; ecstasy." I think these definitions describe how the male trance seems to many women.

There is something both very different and yet very familiar about considering men in this way. It is *familiar* to women in that often men seem not to know what's going on around them. It's also *different* because we don't usually think about the trance as being an active state, a real adaptive stance, a distinct state of mind.

The trance serves many of the same purposes as structure. In a way, men's structure allows the trance to occur. However, the specific value of the trance is to *filter out*, to remove from awareness. To understand this better, we will return to thinking about the little boy and his mother—because the main stimuli that are filtered out are caused by women.

WHAT, ME WORRY?

As Ann talks more about her loneliness with Tony, the story of his trances begins to unfold. It seems to be another example of what may happen when the mother is primarily responsible for parenting.

Tony comes from a pretty traditional family. His father was very well respected in the community, often holding honorary positions in the city government. He even was elected mayor and served two terms. This, of course, kept him away from home even more than his full-time career would have. But everybody liked him, and his family was proud of him. He was a great guy. But his children spent very little time with this great guy, mostly on their annual camping vacations. So for them, their father was absent, his everyday activities were out of view, and they didn't know much about how he actually got along with people in relationships.

Initially, none of this was a problem for Tony's mother.

She had wanted to live a traditional life. Her husband's financial success made it possible for her to enjoy her time at home with her children and she was very involved with them, planning educational activities for them, teaching them to read, supporting and loving them.

But after a while, the situation began to wear on her. She began to feel overloaded with all the household and child-care responsibilities. And gradually, she began to get angry. But who could complain? Her husband was the most admired man in the community, other women were clearly envious of her, and she didn't want to tarnish his reputation (or hers) by complaining to her friends. So she kept the anger inside and even tried to deny that it was there.

But her anger did come out. She sort of complained all the time. It wasn't bitter or loud, but it was constant. She did it only at home, so the children were the only ones who heard it. In time, she began to feel overwhelmed with all of her responsibilities. So she had less and less patience with her children. She became very bossy and demanding. It was clear that she was in charge at home, that her husband was a kind of visitor.

Tony hated this. He admired his father as much as anyone else, and he wanted to think of him as being as strong at home as he was in the world. He had gotten used to spending a lot of time with his mother. But her domineering style and complaining about his father were intolerable to Tony. Not only did it ruin his image of his father, it made it impossible for Tony to get a good sense of his father as a man. This in turn made it impossible for him to get a good sense of himself as a man.

Tony began to tune his mother out. He could be with her all day without really hearing a word she said. He could fantasize about being on a camping trip or picture himself as running his own company. He could even make his mind go completely blank. In this state, he could make brief, automatic responses, and he was completely comfortable. The tension caused by his mother's chronic unhappiness was gone. There wasn't anything that Tony could do about what his mother said, but he had discovered a way to keep it from affecting him. He could just mentally go away.

Tony's mother hated this behavior in Tony. She never could tell if she had his attention, because his facial expression didn't change. He regularly forgot things. This behavior led her to see him as stupid, and she would hound him about his schoolwork. How would he ever amount to anything if he couldn't even think straight? How would he be able to be successful, like his father, as everyone expected him to be, if he was so distracted? He was almost an embarrassment.

But Tony felt safe. He knew that things were not really all right, that he was avoiding something. He knew that his mother was angry. He knew that he looked stupid and irresponsible. But once he had discovered this soothing state, it was impossible to leave. In fact, his mother's complaints about him became as easy to ignore as anything else she said. It was as if she wasn't criticizing him at all.

This state made every emotional pain recede so far into the distance that it was no longer noticeable.

Tony's mother's behavior may seem extreme, and Tony's adaptation, therefore, unusual. But this is not really so. What is really very common is that men get into the trance to filter out the stimuli created by women. Another look back at childhood helps us understand this.

Remember that when the little boy is growing up, he is surrounded by the world of women. Around him are female things, female ways of talking, female ways of doing and, of course, of *feeling*. As he is becoming aware of his difference from females, the boy is learning the ways to *be* different than they are. So he will need to act and feel in different ways. In fact, to feel "female" feelings or to "act like a girl" is dangerous for a boy who is becoming a man. They are not the ways that a boy is supposed to be. That is, a boy is supposed to be not-female, not-Mother.

It would be impossible for the boy to screen and evaluate all of the stimuli coming in from females (especially Mother), to determine whether or not they are acceptable male behavior and then to accept them or reject them. Even if the young boy had the ability to figure this out (which is beyond him), it would take most of his waking energy to do it. It is much more efficient to block *all* stimuli out of consciousness at the start. Most boys learn to do this, and this is perhaps the earliest form of the trance.

In screening out feminine stimuli, the boy finds that a whole set of distractions to his masculinity are filtered out. This makes it much easier to concentrate on, to listen to, the masculine. It makes it easier to feel masculine. This perpetuates the experience of men as comrades, as buddies, and of women as "other."

As the little boy is learning how to be a grown-up man, he learns to be not-female, and then he begins to learn the concrete things that will make him masculine. But many of those things are external things, like rules or codes of behavior, things like *always compete to win, never let them see your fear, don't cry, fight for your team,* and even *never let a woman tell you what to do.* These rules describe behavior, action, or appearance, but they don't say anything about what is inside the person, motivating these behaviors. While very specific and definite about behavior, they don't say anything about how a person who is behaving in these ways might *feel,* which is precisely the point! That is, these rules make it unnecessary to feel. They also make it unnecessary for the boy to learn much about how he feels and what to do about feelings.

This leaves the boy still vulnerable to his feelings. He knows how to act, how to give the appearance to himself and to others that he is in control. Most important, he knows how to look like a man. But this is in appearance only. He knows how to act like a man, but this does not mean that he knows how to feel like a man. My husband, for example, could teach his sons what it looked like to kill bugs bravely, but his feelings were very different. In fact, most of the men who have taught him how to act like a man have themselves learned about acting like a man but not about feeling like a man. So they can only teach him to avoid the problem.

In addition, since part of acting like a man includes being strong and assured, the boy doesn't learn that grown men can feel insecure, too. So the boy thinks that the adult men really do feel secure about themselves as men. He thinks he is the only one who is uncertain about himself—and he had better keep that to himself, so that no one finds out how he feels. Most men live their whole lives this way.

This is supposed to be a secret, and we're not supposed to say anything about it. But as Mark Twain wrote, "A boy starts acting like a man when he is twelve, and he goes on acting for the rest of his life." We all buy the act.

This gives us a picture of a fragile masculine self-image. It is one that is based on behavior and appearances, but lacking in confidence. But this appearance may be all that a man has of his masculine identity. His sense of himself depends on this appearance. He doesn't have much else to use. He hasn't learned how to use his feelings to understand himself—his reactions, needs, fears, or desires.

Therefore, when it comes to the world of emotions, he is at a loss. He has not learned how to understand and maneuver in this world. After all, this is the feminine world, an area to be avoided. A man is supposed to be competent. But in the world of feelings, he actually is incompetent. And if he is confronted with having to deal with feelings, he feels inept.

Of course, it is not acceptable to be incompetent. To be considered competent or to consider himself as competent, he must regain control. To do so, he must eliminate from his world any input that makes him feel out of control. That means he must invalidate to himself the importance of feelings. He must cut himself off from the world of feelings, which is the women's domain.

In addition, because his role model demands of him only male "behaviors," he must distance himself from all things female, such as looks, gestures, and emotional responses. They do not count, they have no importance. In fact, they must be screened out to allow the sense of self to be intact. The realm of feelings is a part of women's experience that must be screened out. Other realms also fall into this category, partly determined by a man's particular culture, such as being concerned about the children, being aware of food or entertainment needs, noticing how things look, keeping track of the whereabouts and activities of various family members, remembering birthdays and events that are meaningful to other people. These activities and concerns are usually all female, and a man then learns to screen them out.

The trance state accomplishes all of this. When he is in this state, a man can filter out most of the day-to-day activities and feelings going on around him. How common it is for a woman to ask a man to do something, for him even to repeat back to her what he agreed to do, and a few hours later for him to deny he's ever heard anything about it. Many men never hear anything when they're watching TV. It's not atypical for a woman to hear the complaint, about something a man is unaware of, "But you told me that when I was sleeping." She had actually talked to him when he was awake, but clearly tuned very far out.

If someone is upset about something, a man in the

trance doesn't notice or feel it. It is as if it isn't happening, as if it just doesn't exist. If someone needs something, he isn't aware of it. He doesn't have to feel inadequate in those circumstances, as he might if he were aware of them.

It is also important to note that because he has not learned to understand and deal with feelings, including his own, he is at risk if painful feelings should impinge on him. Without ways of coping with these feelings, he feels overwhelmed, frightened, lost, and vulnerable if he is in touch with them. The trance keeps him from feeling, and so it protects him from all this.

THE SECRET LIFE OF WALTER MITTY

James Thurber's Walter Mitty was a less than ordinary guy. He was shy, self-conscious, and a bumbler. But he had an elaborate fantasy life. In these fantasies, his "secret life," he was the bravest, most attractive, most successful, and most intelligent of men. No wonder he preferred that world to the real one.

Tony's father was a real man, a success. He was everything a man was supposed to be. How was Tony ever going to be like him? Compared to him, how was he going to feel anything but inadequate? Through the trance, naturally! When he's in the trance, he can feel as powerful as he needs to feel, because the feeling of inadequacy is blocked out.

The image that men have of what they should be is impossible to attain in reality. I know that we women have our unrealistic goals, too, most painfully in expecting ourselves to be perfect mothers. The goals that men are supposed to achieve are big goals in the big world. These expectations are pumped up, glorified, and held out as real, achievable accomplishments.

A man is supposed to be successful in his career and make a lot of money. This is supposed to be done at only reasonable personal cost and effort. That is, he should not complain, and his job should not appear to be too hard for him. His strength and competency should show in the ease with which he accomplishes the superior or extraordinary.

He must look calm and contained in his own world. He should maintain the image of masculine omnipotence. He should always know the answer and know what to do. (How often do you hear a man comfortably say, "I don't know"?) He should not get thrown by other people's feelings and needs. He should not experience helplessness or insecurity in himself.

How does he accomplish this? He doesn't see or hear. He is in his own private world, where everything is coherent and understandable. If he breaks the trance, he is vulnerable to the pain of reality.

In his fantasy, like Walter Mitty, he is everything he is supposed to be. He handles emergencies smoothly; he impresses everybody; he never disappoints anybody, including himself. He always comes through like a hero. In the trance, he is in his own fantasy world where he is strong, brave, courageous, and always, always competent.

While he is feeling strong and brave in his own private

world, though, here you and I are, handling the messes of everyday life. He acts for all the world like he is above all of this. It is as if he doesn't care about it, as if he takes all of it—the house, the social obligations, the children—for granted. If the roof started leaking, he probably would just put on a raincoat! Since our image of men is the same as the one they have of themselves, capable and competent, that is the framework we use to understand their behavior. So if a strong, capable man doesn't do what needs to be done, it looks to us like lack of concern, or just plain laziness. If we realize, though, that he doesn't know all that we think he knows, his behavior makes more sense.

I know, I know. This is easier said than done. I always ask my husband questions as if he actually knows the answer. I act as if I am still a little girl, and he is my daddy, and I think he knows everything about the world. It's crazy. Yes, my husband knows a lot about math and about current world events and political science. But I had a much broader education than he did. Yet I am likely to ask him questions like, "How long will it take them to repair the roof?" or "Why is rain still leaking into the basement?" or even "Why does the government keep underestimating the federal deficit?" then I catch myself. *Be serious!* But when I am asking the questions, I truly believe that he is going to have the answers. We expect this of men. And we probably all contribute to pushing men into the trance by expecting them to live Walter Mitty's secret life for real.

It is difficult for us to be empathic to the problems that the trance solves, when we often feel like the victims of it. This is because a man is most likely to slip into the trance in his relationships with important women. The important woman, especially the wife, has the kind of importance to a man, and therefore holds the same kind of power over him, that the omnipotent mother held over the little boy. It is precisely *because* she is so important to him that the man shields himself against her. ("The doctor says you should talk into my left ear.")

The woman's smile means everything to him. It is all-important that she be pleased with him. To him, her anger and disappointment mean the end of everything. One Vietnam veteran I know said that he would "rather face the Cong than my wife when she's angry." This ongoing fear constitutes too vulnerable a state for the man to experience continuously. So he enters the trance and is safe. He can be with the woman without being frightened about what is happening between them. He can have the relationship without fear and uncertainty accompanying it.

Note that Tony isn't in the trance when he's out in the world. He is well-liked, is a clever conversationalist and is able to be attentive to and interested in others. But when he comes home, he sits in front of the television (a wonderful trance-inducer). He reads the newspaper and feels satisfied and safe in the knowledge that Ann is nearby, yet emotionally at a safe distance from him.

Ann likes to talk. Like most women, she organizes her thoughts and feelings by talking something through, out loud, with another person. And, as with most women, Ann's impulse, when Tony comes home, is to greet him with "How was your day?"—a pleasant, open-ended question, indicating caring and interest. Right? Not to Tony. To him it means, among other things, "Were you successful?" (that is, were you a good-enough man?) "How are you feeling?" and "Tell me something that will make me happy." These may as well be post-hypnotic suggestions to Tony to enter the trance.

Tony usually answers, "Oh, it was okay" to Ann's question. Then he heads for the television, needing to evade what feels like Ann's neediness or scrutiny, eager to enter safe territory.

For Ann it is very painful to be with Tony, whom she loves, and experience him as distant, unreachable, even evasive. But this state, which is so painful for her, is safe for him. Ironically, it is only because of Ann's importance to Tony that he is so far away. He is worried that he is not successful enough at his career for her, that he can't answer her questions about how he is feeling, that he can't please her.

Ann can't make Tony give up the trance. He's used it since he was a young boy, it has served him well, and the dangers that lead him to go into it are still present. But she can be aware of it and do some things differently, with the understanding that what seems innocent and harmless to her is not so to him. Her response to this information can change the way Tony feels when he comes home; it can affect how often, how automatically, and how quickly he enters his trance.

For example, when Tony comes in the door, instead of immediately trying to engage him, Ann might just say, "Hello, I'm glad you're home." Then she can let him know that she'll be upstairs with the kids, or in the kitchen attending to something for dinner, or pulling a few weeds out in the yard. Where and what don't matter. If he knows that she's all right and occupied, he doesn't feel so threatened by the sense that she *needs* him right now. He gets a chance to settle in, to make the transition from work to home, to watch the news. If it feels safe, he may not need to be in his trance all evening. He can then approach her.

Similarly, if Ann comes home after Tony and finds him already engrossed in the newspaper and television, she shouldn't expect him to put them aside at once to be with her. It doesn't matter that that is what *she* would do, were the situation reversed. She is different than he is. She can let him know it's good to see him, she can even tell him she would like to talk with him and ask him what would be a good time. He's likely to answer that he'd like to finish the news. That ought to be okay with Ann; nowhere is it written that there is an absolute rule that the one correct way to behave under the circumstances is to jump up and greet the other person. That may be the correct behavior in one culture and entirely irrelevant in another.

For example, when we had some guests from the Soviet Union arrive at our home from the airport, I offered a choice of snacks and drinks. I got no response, and so I offered again. Still there was no response, but I could see that they were uncomfortable. One of our guests was insightful and sensitive enough to explain, "That is not how we behave in the Soviet Union. We are the guests. We should not choose what you are going to offer us. You decide." There I was, thinking that I was being thoughtful and generous, when they felt put on the spot!

There are no guaranteed methods for dealing with the trance. It won't go away. It's built in to men's nervous systems. It's a habit, and it's also a marvelous feeling. It's like a state of self-hypnosis, like being safe and protected in a cocoon. (You should try it sometime, if you can!) But the harder you fight it, the more intense it becomes. If you understand it, you can work around it creatively. If you understand the man's vulnerabilities, you can avoid producing what feels to him like a frontal attack. And if he's not under attack, he doesn't have to be as defensive, and you won't seem as much like the enemy.

For example, if you were to criticize Ed for his ambidextrous remote control habit, he's more likely to get a third gadget than to say, "You're right, dear, it is a bit much, isn't it?" Consider him gone when he's tuned in to his TV. Don't say anything important to him when you know he can't hear you. Connie, on the other hand, is going to continue to have a hard time with Chuck, but mostly if she expects him to be different. He doesn't know how. He doesn't even really know what he's doing or how painful it is to Connie.

It takes effort to see a man taking care of himself instead of trying to get away from you, but it's worth it. You grow less angry and defensive, and therefore you have a lot more flexibility. You can be more creative about how to deal with someone if you are not in a panic about whether or not he loves or cares about you. Because the fact of the matter is that though the trance is triggered by your style of communicating, and by your importance to him, it is really about him, not about you.

Chapter Five

OTHER MEN

A very small ad ran in the *London Times* in 1909. It said: "Men wanted for hazardous journey. Small wages. Bitter cold. Long months of complete boredom. Constant danger. Safe return doubtful. Honor and recognition in case of success."

The ad was run by Ernest Shackelton, who was organizing an expedition to the South Pole. Thousands of men responded to this ad, willing to give up everything, including their lives, for the privilege of joining this expedition. Honor and recognition would result from the willingness and ability to face and survive "constant danger."

Bud had just turned sixteen. He was a real man, now, he thought. Things that used to frighten him wouldn't bother him anymore. There probably wasn't much of anything he couldn't handle. Such was the mood he was in the day that he and his best friend went to Six Flags amusement park.

Bud had been on the parachute ride two years earlier, and he'd been utterly terrified. There he was, held up by a couple of flimsy straps as the machine lifted him up high enough, he thought, to see the state line! And then the machine apparently let him free-fall until the chute suddenly caught the air. He couldn't even remember that. He hadn't exactly lost consciousness, but he had been so frightened that he had lost all memory of it.

As he and Tom approached the ride this time, however, he was fearless. No problem, he thought. I'll show Tom how this is done. They stood in line, joking, until it was their turn. But strapped into that flimsy seat, Bud's old fear started to return. As he was lifted up higher and higher, fear turned to terror. And this time, he felt the sudden drop, his stomach seeming to stay in his throat.

"Wasn't that great?" yelled Tom, as they got off the ride. "Let's go up again."

"Sure," agreed Bud. "But let's go eat now. I'm starved." He felt so stupid for thinking that his fear would just go away. But he wouldn't let anyone else know. Twenty years later, he went on the same ride with his kids. He was still scared, but they never knew how much. Fathers don't let on with their kids that they are scared.

There are some vitally important things that men simply cannot get from women, just as there are things that we as women cannot get from men. There is a man's man, and there is a woman's man, and they are not the same thing. The main loves in their lives may be women. But men's masculine self-esteem rests on the approval of other men.

We as women are usually focused on men in relation

to ourselves. That is, we see men in terms of whether they are of interest to us, how they meet our needs, whether we feel good when we are around them, whether their behavior fits with our values. We see men in terms of our world, and are not part of the private world that men share together. (The opposite of this is, of course, also true; men are not part of our private world.) Because of this, we usually have a limited view of what men mean to one another. And much of what we see is so "coded" as to be invisible to us.

Brad was a middle-aged man with boyish good looks and an energetic manner. He came to see me for therapy when he was at a crisis point in his life.

He felt he had run out of "macho." He was experiencing symptoms of severe anxiety as he realized that he could not just "do anything," no matter how difficult or stressful. What unfolded as he told his story was that his symptoms had begun when he had lost his father, or, more specifically, when he had lost the *image* of his father.

Brad's father was a special father-figure for everyone who knew him. He was strong and wise; his manner was firm, solid, and self-assured. He could answer any question, solve any problem. He always knew the right thing to do. He was calm and unruffled in any crisis.

But Brad had discovered something that had been a family secret. In the context of someone else in the family having trouble, an uncle had told Brad that appearances to the contrary, his father had *not* been able to handle all that came his way. In fact, his father had been plagued by severe symptoms of anxiety, which he had scrupulously hidden from almost everyone. Most of the family, including Brad, knew his father as a pillar of strength, the one to whom everyone turned in a crisis, a calm and dependable source of wisdom and guidance. But this was only what appeared on the surface. Underneath, it turned out, his father had always felt frightened and anxious. He suffered from depression, panic attacks, phobias, and compulsive behaviors.

Brad had to alter his image of his father. In doing this, he had lost the linchpin of his masculine identity. This left him, too, feeling frightened and unsettled. He had modeled himself after his father. He had admired his father greatly and feared him as well. Since his father was so wise and competent, his thinking badly of Brad would have felt devastating. Consequently, he always tried to be the kind of man his father was, the kind of man he was supposed to be.

The news about his father was crushing. Brad didn't know how to behave or what to think anymore, since his model had turned out to be a false image. What else had he counted on, he wondered, that was now uncertain or false? At this point in his therapy, I referred him to a men's therapy group. I think that all the empathy and understanding in the world, coming from a woman, could not replace what he had lost. He could not rebuild the foundation of his masculinity without support and input from other men.

ONE OF THE BOYS

More than any other part of this book, this chapter is "hearsay." I have had to be part of the private world of men to know as much as I know. I have talked with many men, asked many questions, and done much listening. But even then men are telling me things, sharing with *me*, as a woman. And since I am a woman, they can't be with me the way that they can other men. But even though I am not a part of that private world, I think that I have gained a working understanding of what it means, and that is what I will share with you.

This world is foreign to us as women. An experience from our men's and women's study group dramatizes this. We had done just about all we could to try to understand the opposite sex by reading professional literature, and we were finding it more productive to learn from each other's personal experiences. The women in the group said that it was our observation that men did not really seem to share much feeling with each other, that their relationships seemed emotionless. One of the men jumped in to say that he had an example to give of how emotional men could be with each other. We women were literally on the edge of our seats. We were just dying to hear this.

"Well, our men's group had been meeting for almost three years. We always met at the same time and place for an hour and a half. We decided to have a get-together somewhere else so that we could really spend some time with each other. We met at one guy's apartment complex and had a barbecue around the pool. We spent the whole afternoon together."

His voice was full of emotion; he was excited about being able to share this important moment with the group. "But the part I remember the most, the part where we had this incredible closeness with each other that I'll never forget, was this great game of water polo!" He sat back with a very pleased look on his face.

"That's it?" we said, absolutely stunned. "That's the *whole story*?" Our worst fears had been confirmed: Men really *don't* have feelings. But we pushed on and asked a few more questions.

The man telling the story didn't really have much else to say, except that he and his friends in the group would always remember that afternoon as one of the most wonderful times in their lives. It had solidified their relationships with each other. It had been *full* of meaning and feeling—wordless, uncomplicated connectedness.

This example illustrates how men's experience with each other is different from women's experience with other women. We simply cannot use our own experience with each other to try to understand men's relationships with other men. If we do, we won't be able to understand this example, and we can't understand men.

One of the key differences between women and men is in what we each need from others for our sense of self-esteem and identity. We women can get a sense of our identity from our mothers. Whether or not we like what we get, there is a clear and simple path for us to get a dependable sense of our femininity: our continuous connection with and similarity to our mothers. The task of forging an identity (specifically a gender identity) is more circuitous for men. Because men's connections with their fathers are almost always less immediate and continuous than our relationships with our mothers, men learn how to be men through concrete input from outside of themselves. And that input has to come from those who know—from other men.

To be "one of the boys" means to be accepted—and acceptable. Without this seal of approval from other men, a boy or a man has serious doubts about his masculinity. Since his masculine identity is achieved through concrete behaviors and actions, his acceptability can be measured. To be a man, he has to do things the way men do them. The saying "Real men don't eat quiche" was meant as a joke, but it would not have been humorous had it not contained a lot of truth. If he does things the way other men do them, a man will probably gain their approval, and, if he is really lucky, their admiration.

My husband tells a story from his childhood that illustrates this point vividly. Part of a large family, and sandwiched between two sisters, he spent plenty of time with girls. He learned to play jacks, hopscotch, and jump rope. He says that he was pretty good. When he was about eight, he was out on the playground at school when the girls asked the boys if they wanted to join a game of jump rope. My husband was eager to play, since he knew how. Several boys went first, trying clumsily the way boys do, and "missing" right away. George was proud to take his turn; knowing how well he'd do, he was looking forward to the excitement and praise his performance would bring. He started jumping, with light, bouncy jumps, the way girls do.

But the response was silence. Something was terribly wrong. George realized very quickly that it was not acceptable for him to jump rope differently from the other boys. His skill at a girls' game was not only not admirable, it was embarrassing. Within seconds, he took the bounce out of his jump and landed on the rope. It was a lesson well learned and never forgotten. To be one of the boys, do things the way all the other boys do them.

It is with his peers that the boy learns most about "correct" masculine behavior. The young boy has spent considerable physical and emotional energy trying to be like Dad, to win his father's approval. He may try to hit a lot of home runs, be smart in school, or win a lot of fights to show how strong he is. But most men end up feeling that they never really get this approval. They turn to other men as a substitute, an action they continue throughout life.

THE MISSING FATHER, AGAIN

As he is growing up, the boy attempts to identify with his father. This basically means that he wants to act like his father, look like his father, and do the things that his father does. But this is not an easy matter, and there are a number of hurdles to overcome.

First of all, the father has often been relatively absent. Consequently, many of his actions take place away from the boy and so are invisible or mysterious. The boy does not have a lot of real connection with his father, with his physical presence, his emotional substance. And because the father usually acts like a man, and doesn't express much emotion, there is not much feeling between them. This makes it even more unlikely that the boy will be able to feel an emotional connection, a real sense of emotional nurturing, on a deep level.

Secondly, fathers, like all parents, tend to forget what it was like to be a small boy. They just want their sons to do the best they can, and when they respond to them, it is often with an expectation that they can do more or better. They seldom think to give approval for how the boy actually is. The expectation for males in our society is that they be capable. Helplessness, fear, and uncertainty, which are natural parts of childhood, are not acceptable parts of maleness. So not only fathers, but all of us, tend to react negatively when we see those things in boys.

I remember always feeling sorry for my brother after he had mowed the lawn. (That was his job, not mine. I still don't do it very well!) My father was never pleased with his work and always went over the places that he had missed. Now, I know that my brother didn't do that great a job. But he was probably all of ten years old. And besides, why should he want to? After all, nothing he did was ever good enough.

Brad, too, was in a terrible position. His father was one of those men whom everybody admired. Within their circle of family and close friends, he was the one everyone turned to for advice. He was calm and wise and had a solution for every problem; he was careful and meticulous in his work and never made mistakes. Although his wife had a terrible temper, he never lost his, and he was always there to take care of the children if she just couldn't manage.

Brad felt that he could never live up to this image of his father, but it was his obligation to try. His family didn't think that he would be much of a success in life. He got into fights at school and was not a very good student. He was his father's first son, so he was supposed to carry on his father's success. Yet no one could possibly accomplish this. Brad wanted to prove to all of them that he could. He wanted their acceptance and their praise.

When he found things difficult, he thought that he shouldn't find them so because his father would not have. He would have been capable and calm. He criticized himself mercilessly for all his failings and was a relentless perfectionist. And he punished himself as much for his feelings as for his failings. Everything he did was in an attempt to be just as good as his father.

When he found out that his father had had anxiety attacks, he began to have them too. Probably a part of this was an unconscious identification with that part of his father, his automatic attempt to be just like him. But another part was the undermining of his whole definition of himself. He had modeled himself after this ideal of masculinity, strong and fearless. Now he found out that it was an illusion. So what could he model himself after? He was left truly terrified, with no idea of how to be the right kind of man. He was like a ship with no rudder.

Brad's dilemma is a specific example of the more general problem: because fathers are distant, mysterious, critical, and, in a sense, untouchable, the growing boy is deprived of a direct route to masculine self-esteem.

MASCULINE IDENTITY IS PRECARIOUS

How, then, does the boy develop a good, solid sense of himself? The sad reality is that he usually doesn't. The identification with Father is left incomplete, and the boy leaves childhood with a precarious sense of his masculinity.

The boy, and then the man, needs constant input to reassure him of his masculinity. The need for the father's recognition and approval is transferred to other men. The man continues to need an important connection with the world of men.

What can be very reassuring about this masculine world is that the rules are spelled out pretty clearly. Some examples of the rules, and these should be getting easy to figure out by now, are don't smile too much, don't look as if you need anyone's approval, always appear confident, act like you know what you are doing at all times, don't say that you don't know or that you can't, don't show your feelings, don't appear to need anybody, always play to win, be a team player, never turn and run, don't cry, don't be a sissy, earn a lot of money, be strong, don't complain, follow your leader's orders, and women and children first.

These rules provide security for men, but they often sound frightening to me. When, for example, I was listening to a recent radio report about an earthquake, some men were preparing to re-enter a building that was threatening to collapse. They were quoted as saying, "Being good men, we'll continue in spite of the risk." It sounds just like the expedition to the Antarctic: "... hazardous journey. Small wages.... Constant danger.... *Honor and recognition in case of success.*"

If he follows the rules (like "keep going in spite of the risk"), a man can be pretty sure that he is doing things acceptably. If he breaks away, he is never sure. And if he does something that is considered feminine, surely he is likely to be labeled as unmanly, by other men—because there is nothing less manly than something that is womanly! And since he depends on this outside opinion for this masculine sense of himself, being viewed as unmanly makes him unmanly.

Anything emotional is feminine. Any desire for closeness is feminine. Here we find an interesting paradox. On the one hand, men need each other continuously in order to feel good about themselves. On the other hand, they are not supposed to have any real emotional feeling about each other. That would be feminine, out of bounds. Inappropriate emotionality gets a boy labeled as a "sissy" and a man labeled as "effeminate." Men have to have acceptable, "masculine" ways to express and experience their closeness with and attachment to each other.

Overt emotional or physical closeness with men is outside the rules. In fact, fear of homosexuality is quite real to a lot of men, believing that if they let themselves feel that they care, or show that they care about another man, especially physically, then they have lost their masculinity. Many men then equate this with homosexuality, believing that homosexuality means loss of masculinity. Rules and limits on this behavior keep men safe from these fears.

Men can express their caring for each other through carefully defined and limited behaviors. The cues are usually nonverbal. A nod of the head, a glance of the eye, or even a punch on the arm will suffice. Physical contact is allowed only during sports. (Don't forget, athletes are strong, competitive men, real men, with no apparent doubts about their masculinity.) Within the defined bounds, the essential contact with other men is allowed.

The code is quite subtle. Here's a favorite story that illustrates this point. A man and a woman who are just getting to know each other are out for a jog. A woman jogger approaches them, and the woman in the couple stops, greets the other woman warmly, and they embrace. Shortly after they start running again, a man approaches the couple. The man in the couple doesn't change his stride, but makes a small wave with his right hand.

"Who was that woman?" asks the man.

"Oh, nobody special, just someone I know from a book club I was in a few years ago. Who was that guy?"

"I was best man at his wedding last month."

Or, as another example, two male college roommates could meet after not seeing each other for ten years. The greeting might be, "Are you still wearing that mangy coat? You just don't want anybody knowing how you're raking it in! And you still don't have any taste, do you?"

We women just don't do it the same way, do we? We

would squeal with delight, embrace, and say something like, "It is *so* good to see you. I can't believe it's you. You look *fantastic*. We have *so* much to talk about. I want to know everything that's happened to you!"

THE PRIVATE WORLD OF MEN

If we suspend our value judgments and preconceptions, perhaps we can look more empathically at the private world of men and understand more accurately what they gain from each other. Their behaviors usually meet their emotional needs, even though the behaviors and the needs are often different from ours. Whereas we might operate in the worlds of feelings, caretaking, child care, homemaking, fashion, or the attractiveness or appeal of our environment, men operate in other worlds.

I'm sure that what everyone thinks of first in this regard is the sports world. There are rules to follow, a team to be a part of, a competition to be won, a hero to be admired. There is plenty for men to talk about together without having to be personal. As awkward and uncomfortable as you might feel, if you can talk about the latest game, the home team, or someone's outstanding performance, you can make contact. And one important point to make here is that in playing sports, closeness through physical contact is allowed. In fact, the world of sports is so important that I've devoted a whole chapter to it.

There are other worlds men share—like the hardware store club. Yes, I'm serious. Men can talk for hours about drill bits and wrenches, and nails and screws. (Do you know how many different *kinds* of screws there are, to say nothing of the many sizes of each kind?) Everything is measured and calculated. There are countless tools, each for a special purpose, and each carefully designed and calibrated. This world has lots of structure, no feelings, and everyone can talk the same language. Endlessly. And these stores foster the illusion that with the right tools, any man can look truly competent.

Then, too, there's the poker game. In this setting, men show each other how competitive they can be. If a man is invited to join a poker game, he instantly has a sense that he belongs. And most of the time, the game is a regular one, with people he knows and can depend on to be there. It's another way to maintain connections with men without ever having to show a feeling!

Then, of course, there is the military. Most men have extremely fond memories of their days in the service. Although they may have hated it overall, they loved special parts of it. They made friends that they keep for life. In the military, they always know exactly what is expected of them. They don't have to worry about looking foolish, because everyone does the same thing. And they never have to worry about looking feminine, because they are not allowed to do anything remotely feminine! There are plenty of men around to give that strong sense of masculine identity. They can be really very close to each other without worrying about what it means, because they are all required to eat, bathe, dress, sleep, and work together.

Fraternities, too, can be a powerful source of connection

for men. And it is striking how the potential members prove their worthiness to enter the group through intense rushing rituals. Hazing rituals are often seriously dangerous, even life-threatening, but once a member has proven himself, he's in for life.

Real brothers have the potential to be the most important of connections for men. If the threat of closeness seems too great, brothers may remain distant, and even become enemies. But the other possibility is that brothers can be the closest of allies, with the wordless understanding of each other that men find most rewarding.

Then there are exclusive groups, men's organizations that do not allow women. There is ultimate safety in such a setting—a major reason they are so steadfastly and so righteously defended. Of course, such groups also maintain social and political power; only the strongest and best men are able to join certain clubs. This helps the club maintain an image of power and reassures the man who has been admitted that he has really arrived.

Let's not forget about the "boys' night out." Though women may be most aware of what frightens us about these outings, such as too much drinking, or involvement with other women, the most important part of these evenings for men is the connection. One group of men from a major metropolitan area has actually formed a corporation called "We Bad Co." The purpose of the group is to have fun together. They love to call themselves "bad," which lets them be "macho" or masculine, but the "we" is the first and most important part of their name.

Men clearly gain a great deal of security and comfort

from their connections in the world of men. And, again, because they gain this comfort in a form that is different from ours, and therefore not obvious to our eyes, we often tend to demean and devalue it.

Consider the following: I have a female friend who has a regular squash partner. They meet at the same place and same time every week for an hour. Then they change and go out for dinner or coffee. And they talk. The game is an excuse for the relationship. My friend likes squash, but what she really looks forward to is the time to talk with her partner.

A man may have a regular tennis partner for years. When he comes home after an afternoon of tennis, his wife asks, "So, what did you talk about?" The husband says, "Nothing." They just played tennis. They don't want to talk, have to talk, need to talk. They connect through competition with a friend, through returning a serve that should have been an ace, or through a long and excruciatingly demanding rally. They don't have to exchange words; they needn't talk of other parts of life. But their relationship is important to them, and they *never* miss a game.

COMMUNICATION STYLE

It is also valuable to consider men's ways of communicating with each other: it's understood that few words are used and that nonverbal cues are preferable. How different this is from the way we communicate as women. We talk a lot, and our conversation is full of details.

Men don't tend to be verbally expressive. They experience women as going on and on over the same thing for no good reason. For men, if you can say it in few words, then you do. The fewer the better, in fact. And if you can communicate a feeling, especially a positive one, such as caring, trust, or understanding, without any words at all, then the communication has more meaning and is felt as more genuine (and more comfortable). If it can be understood without words at all, then there must be a really good contact between you. At the very least, the important words, the words that are simply understood without needing to be spoken, should be left out.

There is a scene from a "Star Trek" episode that really clarified this idea for me. Captain Kirk has been split into two parts of himself, the good Kirk and the evil Kirk. The only way to get the two parts back together is for Kirk to be "beamed down" and then "beamed up" again in the transporter. But this will be dangerous, and he could die in the process. As the process is about to happen, Kirk looks at Spock, his second in command, his successor, his best friend, and says, "If I don't come back. . . ."

To which Spock replies, with a steady gaze, "Understood, Captain."

That's it! It's beautiful, really. These two people really care for and understand each other—that's all they have to say.

Men don't blab or gossip. I recall a man who was in marital therapy for about ten years. I knew his wife better than I knew him. She would talk about having marital problems, discuss whether she was feeling hopeful or pessimistic, and with her closest friends would share the details. He told no one about their problems until they got a divorce. When you are a man, you just don't talk about those things. They are personal, private, serious, and not shared lightly. In fact, to reveal the emotional problems you have to a third person is not only not proper, it's disloyal. (That is one reason why men typically have difficulty entering therapy.) A man who values a relationship will say little about it, will keep it private. A woman who values a relationship will talk about it, especially its problems, with friends. Because it is valuable, she will talk. Because it is valuable, he will not.

Since closeness is disguised in men, men pound each other on the shoulder to express caring. When they really like each other, they hurl outrageous insults at each other. You have to know the private codes that these behaviors represent to know what they mean.

Understanding how men behave with each other helps us understand how they behave in the world at large, and with us. Brad, for example, the man with anxiety symptoms who was mentioned earlier in this chapter, was driven to be successful according to standards set in the world of men. In this area, it mattered little that his wife was proud of him, that she thought that he was wonderful. In fact, he gradually became more distant from her, not because of anything that she was doing, but because he became more and more preoccupied with his internal pressure to perform, to act, and to have confidence in himself, as a real man. Without knowing the personal meaning to him, she could easily interpret his distance as a personal rejection.

(At the same time, it is useful to remember that what a man does to feel good about himself in his relationships with other men will not usually threaten his relationships with women. In fact, if a man feels strong and clear about himself as a man, he can be more relaxed, more confident, and therefore less threatened in his relationships with women.)

Knowing specifically how men behave with each other makes many things more understandable. It also makes a lot of things that were once boring a lot more interesting. If you watch a Western, for example, look for the cues, the silent nods, the knowing looks. I used to think Westerns were boring—no dialogue. I can appreciate them now. I can see the warmth and the caring and the connection. Men appreciate a loyal *act* more than words and are likely to express their acknowledgment not with words, but with actions. Men do die for each other, after all, and for us, and that's certainly caring.

In fact, I was just watching an old episode of "Gunsmoke." Matt Dillon was questioning a young fellow about a man who has been injured and who has the same last name as the young man.

"Any relation?" Dillon asks.

"Well," says the young man, "he rescued me from a trash heap when I was six days old, has taught me everything he knows, gave me his last name. It would be me lying there like that instead of him if he hadn't thrown himself over me. I guess you'd call that a relationship."

Chapter Six

WORK

Richard is an ophthalmologist, with a special interest in the problems of the elderly. It has never been clear whether or not Richard actually enjoys his work. He gets angry about the prevailing attitude that we should expect vision to deteriorate as people grow old and that therefore there is no need to try to correct these problems. He has a grateful following of elderly patients whose lives have been improved through his efforts. Many of these people are on fixed incomes and have poor insurance coverage, so Richard rarely gets his full fee.

Though his work takes up most of his time and energy, it rarely seems to give Richard much real pleasure. However, whenever there is more work to do, Richard does it. There seems to be no limit on how many hours he will work or how many new patients he will take. He doesn't seem to notice. His wife, Anne, on the other hand, can't help but notice. His work always seems to be a priority for Richard, and Anne feels that she never is.

Richard and Anne live in a lovely home, and their daughter goes to the best private school in the city. Anne's job as a magazine editor gives her plenty of flexibility in her schedule, and she is able to enjoy time with her daughter and to enjoy their home. Though with Richard's busy schedule, they take few vacations, when they do, they certainly travel in style.

Richard considers himself a success, but Anne is complaining. She thinks that Richard is a unique and special individual. She values his commitment to his patients. But she married him because she wanted to be with him, spend time with him, enjoy him, and he is always busy. He feels like a success. She feels like his work is ruining their life.

Maureen couldn't believe how Jon had conned her into going to this movie. "You'll love it," he'd said. "It's romantic. It's all about how much this guy loves this woman." They'd gone, and it turned out to be the most violent, blood-and-guts action adventure movie she'd seen in years.

The movie was *Die Hard.* It starts out with the lead character having to risk life and limb in order to take care of his wife. He's a police officer. Taking care of people is his work. He'll do what he has to do, whatever it takes. He's aware of his wife the whole time he's risking his life and working so hard. When he works, he works for her.

"That's what I mean," said Jon. "*Die Hard*—a love story!"

Steven's father was a police lieutenant, a career officer who was beloved and admired by all. In his community, he was the man on whom everyone could depend through thick and thin. Working his way through the system, though, had required his working a big share of night shifts and overtime. Young Steven would be left in charge during those times as the "man of the house," and he fulfilled his duties proudly. He made sure that he got the job done, just as his dad would have done it.

Steven was an enthusiastic worker when he, in turn, began raising his own family. His wife, Lisa, had a career, too, and when she was offered a promotion in another city, it was an opportunity neither of them could refuse. Steven wanted her to be fulfilled in her career, and he thought he could certainly find something good for himself in their new location. He was, after all, increasingly successful in his work. And Lisa's salary would double within two years, which would be more than enough to support the entire family. It would also be more than Steven had ever made. But for the first nine months in their new city, Steven couldn't find a decent job.

When Steven came to see me for psychotherapy, he felt unable to cope for the first time in his life. He felt inadequate and depressed. His wife was paying all the bills, and he was doing all the shopping and cleaning. Lisa was beginning to ask more questions about his job search, seemed embarrassed when she introduced him, and stopped complimenting him on his excellent housekeeping skills. Steven thought that she was beginning to hint that she didn't feel she was married to a "real" man.

Steven didn't feel much like a real man either. He thought that he should feel okay, even good, about Lisa's success. After all, he was "liberated." But while Steven may have learned about feminism in today's world, he had learned to be a man—a little man—in his father's world. His most solid sense of himself had come from his father, the dedicated worker who could do the job no matter what.

Traditionally, a man's whole way of being, the structure of his life, especially as a husband and a father, has involved working hard at a job and supporting his family. When Steven found himself unable to do this, he felt worthless. He had to reconstruct his whole sense of himself in therapy, because it seemed likely that he would never again earn more money than his wife and that he would continue to handle many of the household and child-care responsibilities.

This is no one's image of who and what a man is supposed to be. A man is his work. A man's success at work defines his self-esteem, in the eyes of both men and women. When this is threatened, his whole sense of himself is threatened. Just as a woman's sense of herself is intertwined with her sense of herself in relationships, so a man's sense of himself is intertwined with his success at work.

THE MEASURE OF A MAN

We measure a man by his work. Maybe we would like to say that we see more than that in a man, that we are not that superficial. Neither do we want to believe that a woman's value is determined by her appearance. But cultural messages are difficult to erase, and resist them though we may try, we are affected by them.

A man measures himself, too, by his work. Let's look at it from his point of view. He sees his father and he wants to be like him. It is almost certain that his father worked. So his image of himself as male, from the very beginning, is of one who works, and of one who does this work "in the world." And since Father probably was not very available, and there's not much else to know about him, it is easy for the boy to focus on father as *someone who goes away to work.*

Things work differently in the ghetto. There, fathers are often absent, may be unemployed and look like failures, or may be involved in illicit activities. So it's unlikely that boys growing up in this setting will measure themselves by their work, and it's more than likely that these boys will have a relatively shaky masculine self-image.

Although things are changing rapidly now, with the majority of families having two parents who work outside the home, this was not the case for most adult men as they grew up. And as the growing boy is learning how to distinguish himself from females, he is likely to see the father's working as distinguishing him from Mother. This adds another level of importance to the boy's identification of himself as someone who works: it makes him more certainly not-female.

In Steven's case, being just like his father was what he wanted most. He loved and admired his father. And his early self-esteem had come from being able to perform a job the way he thought that his father would have. Nothing gave him more solidity or greater pleasure.

As he became an adult, Steven continued to take pride in his work. He loved challenges, which he not only met, but usually exceeded. And like his dad, who had worked his way up through the system, he believed that if he put in enough sustained effort, he would eventually achieve results.

Not being able to find work, then, was shattering to Steven. He was unable to find some other way to feel good about himself. For one thing, he had never needed to do so before—work had always been there. For another, he had no practice. He had not learned to value other parts of himself to nearly the degree that he had learned to value himself as a worker.

In fact, however, Steven had many fine qualities, a number of which had actually contributed to his success at work. He was a basically kind man, who, despite his competitiveness when trying to get a job done, never wanted to hurt anybody, and rarely did. He was a devoted father himself—his positive relationship with his own father had led him to value that role himself. He was a good friend, always available to help. He was friendly and pleasant, respectful of his community and of his religious affiliation. And, as we have already seen, he was a committed and faithful husband who supported his wife in her independent development as a person.

Sounds pretty good, doesn't it? Maybe to us, but not to Steven. To him, those other things are nice, but they don't *really* mean anything. They are feminine traits, after all, or at least not distinctly masculine. So they are not reassuring when it comes to Steven's self-esteem, which is interwoven with his masculinity; since working is an integral part of that, the other things just don't help very much. To Steven, it's the bottom line that counts. And the bottom line is: no job, no man.

Added to that was the fact that Steven was doing all the housework. This increased the trauma considerably. Not only was he not a man, but he was acting like a woman! It was a formula for psychological disaster. Losing a job is the cause of severe depression, alcoholism and drug abuse, and sometimes even suicide in men. Steven was actually doing quite well relative to those extremes; he only felt awful—he didn't act on those feelings.

Recall, too, that a man's self-esteem depends on the approval of other men. And men don't approve of other men staying home and taking care of the kids and the housework. So Steven worried that everyone thought he was not a real man.

One of the earliest things children hear is, "What are you going to be when you grow up?" The answer to this question is not supposed to be "happy," "secure," or even "well-adjusted"! The answer is a career or a job. For boys, that is. Girls are allowed to answer almost anything these days, although it is still most valued, in many circles, for them to say that they want to get married and have children. But boys know that they are the ones who will support this family.

The expectation for the boy is that he will not only work, but will be successful at what he does. The expectations include achievement. The boy just has to be a little soldier about it and accept his responsibilities. Imagine what people would say about him if he said, "When I grow up, I'd like to stay home and raise children." People weren't too pleased when my brother, in the fourth or fifth grade, said that what he wanted to be was "a philosopher." It would be hard to raise a family on that!

In this light, it is easy to understand, for example, Richard's single-minded involvement with his work. The harder he works, the more of a man he is. His unawareness of Anne's distress is also clear. He is, after all, from his perspective, the perfect husband. He provides a comfortable home, opportunities for his child, and a nice life for his wife. What in the world would Anne have to be dissatisfied with? Emotional involvement with her does not enter the picture. For Richard, success at work equals success as a man equals success as a husband.

The need for success at work is so paramount that many men are without inner resources for coping with loss of their work. This becomes a widespread problem in troubled economic times. During layoffs or strikes, men lose their bearings. It's as if they are nobody, nothing, have no value. Their sense of themselves starts to unravel. They often become severely depressed and frequently turn to alcohol. Their dependency on their wives leads to increased discomfort with themselves, to marital tension, and often to family violence.

Other men's difficulty with a man not working probably has something to do with their own anxiety. Men go to work. Period. If a man chooses not to work, or is involved in something nontraditional, other men don't know what sense to make of it. It threatens the status quo. And I would be surprised if it didn't uncomfortably tickle a hidden wish that *they* could stay home and not have to have a traditional job.

I know a couple—a very talented, successful couple— who, when they started a family, each worked half-time. They each worked two and a half days a week at the office, and two and a half days caring for the children. So, for example, half the time the wife would drive the kids to preschool, while the other half of the time, her husband did. They both loved the arrangement.

But it caused some difficulty for the husband. The mothers at the preschool, for example, didn't act very friendly toward him. He tried to develop relationships with them, but usually got the cold shoulder. He found that his friends never talked about what he was doing. They acted as if it weren't happening. His colleagues kept "forgetting" what he was doing. He thought that they couldn't remember because to them it was too different, too outside the established norm, too unmasculine, and it made them nervous. I agree.

And we women, of course, are subject to the same cultural biases as are men. We want a man to be successful at work. We have been taught that our success is determined by the man we are involved with. We ourselves are not valued by our own accomplishments. We were taught to go out and find ourselves a doctor or a lawyer. When we have attached ourselves to a successful man, then we are successful. No wonder Lisa had such difficulty with

Steven's unemployment. It didn't matter what she herself had accomplished; she didn't feel right unless Steven was working. At bottom, neither gender is really comfortable with a nonworking man.

Every now and then my husband and I entertain the board of directors of the small company with which he is involved. I tease us both about his role as corporate executive, with me being the "corporate wife," a pleasant and charming hostess or companion. And you know, as I think about it, it's not just a joke. Deep down, a part of me believes, too, that my success comes from my husband. When we learn these messages throughout our lives, they become difficult to erase.

One additional piece of this cultural message is that for a woman to be truly successful, she has to marry a man who is more successful than she is. So not only is a man's work the measure of a man, it is also, in some sense, the measure of a woman. The pressure is on from all sides for the man to dominate and excel. It would be interesting to see Anne's response if Richard were to cut back on his work. I'm sure she would be happy to have more time with Richard, but I wonder if she wouldn't be a little anxious, too, if his reputation began to pale, and he became just another ophthalmologist.

HOW IMPORTANT IS MONEY?

Silly question, isn't it? Money is *very* important. And it is also very important that it be the man who earns it.

When you measure a man, you can measure him in dollars and cents. And you can rank him against all the other men. He either measures up or he doesn't. It's a black-and-white issue.

As we have seen, earning money is important to men as a way to feel reassured about their success as men and therefore about their masculine identity. But this is also a hot and complicated issue in relationships between men and women. We are all a part of this problem.

My husband was in the process of a long divorce when I began to date him. He had been married for a long time, had raised his children, and had sent them all to college. He wasn't in great shape financially. But he thought he wouldn't be in any worse shape after the divorce. Well, he misjudged. (Physicians do have a notoriously hard time of it when it comes to divorce settlements.) What we thought would be our future financial life together never materialized. He sometimes couldn't pay his share of our joint expenses.

Now, I have a pretty good career myself. I have always worked and always supported myself. On my own, I have been able to provide for myself a home, a new car when I need one, pleasant vacations, and an adequate, though not impressive, retirement plan. I *never* expected, or wanted, a man to take care of me. Or so I thought.

But I have been disappointed in my husband's financial status. Granted, a part of it is that it isn't what I thought it would be. But a part of it, too, is that he can't take care of me. I have friends who are married to physicians, and they don't have to work as hard as I do. (I cringe when I write this, but it's the truth.) Here I am, an enlightened woman who believes that women are happier when they work and when they earn their own money. I believe that men earning most of the money leads to difficulties in relationships. And yet I have found that this toxic kernel keeps popping up on its own, making me feel cheated. And there's another scary part to this. We as women have been trained for so long that our value is determined by our men, that I am afraid that having a husband who can't support me means that *I* am not valuable.

So we all contribute to the pressure on men to earn money. They need it for their self-esteem. And *we* need it for *our* self-esteem. With so much riding on money, it's no wonder that it is the source of so many conflicts in relationships. For example, it's fairly common for men to earn most of the money, to think they know much better than women how to handle money, and to control all the money in a family or relationship. And it's also common for couples to have a great deal of difficulty sorting this out together.

WHEN IN DOUBT, WORK HARDER

When we are in conflict, we are under stress. When we are under stress, we retreat to the familiar, the safe, the comfortable. So, when a man or a woman is in conflict, each calls on the strategy that will make him or her feel better. This is rarely a conscious choice. Rather, it is based on past experiences and learning and is more reactive than deliberate.

Susie wants a new house. She feels she is entitled to one, and who's to say that this isn't true? But the problem is, she expects Jim to buy her this new house. And he agrees that they should move. But he doesn't think that now is the right time.

Susie isn't exactly traditional. She worked long into the marriage, including while she bore and raised their children. She enjoyed what she did, though of course it was difficult to work full-time and take care of the children. The turning point came when her boss, Louise, resigned. Until Louise left, Susie hadn't realized what an important part of the job she was. Without her, work became extremely difficult, more tiring than usual. And when the new boss arrived, all the reward went out of it. Susie was very experienced at what she did. The new boss didn't delegate very well and tended to look over everyone's shoulder. Susie didn't feel she was really doing her own work anymore. She began to consider quitting.

Jim and Susie talked it over. Susie staying home would eliminate most of the child-care expenses. And Jim was doing quite well himself. They could definitely live comfortably on his salary alone. They agreed that Susie would resign.

Initially, she was relieved to leave the job and delighted to have more time with her children, especially in the summertime. But after a few years, she got caught up in the culture of the other women who were at home. She thought that she should have some new carpeting; they had had the same carpeting since they had bought the house, and she was embarrassed by the stains in front of the sofa. She realized that her clothes weren't very stylish. She began to buy expensive clothes again, despite her long-held belief that she should only buy expensive clothes for work. She was very proud of Jim and his success, and she thought that their lifestyle didn't reflect this. A newer, bigger house would reflect more accurately and favorably on them. Besides, the children were getting bigger, and each of them should have a room of his and her own.

In fact, Jim was doing very well for himself. But the industry in which he worked was a very volatile one. Whatever his local success, there was no guarantee that the company would survive. Buy-outs, both hostile and friendly, were always in the wind. Jim was saving for the possibility that he might be out of work at any moment, through no fault of his own.

But he was in conflict. He wanted his success to show, too. And he wanted Susie to be happy. She was a loving wife, his best friend, and if she wanted a new house, he thought he should make it possible for her to have one. It was up to him.

They bought the new house, and it was truly lovely. Jim fixed up one of the bedrooms as an office. He could use it as a tax deduction. And he began participating in a pyramidal sales program to earn extra money to cover their increased expenses.

Susie was pleased. But a vicious cycle had begun. With the new house, they needed new furniture and drapes, a fence for the backyard, and membership dues at the local swim club so that the children could be with their new neighborhood friends. Jim worked harder at his full-time job and then spent most of the weekends selling. Susie saw less and less of him.

Susie felt confused, irritated, and lonely. Where was her husband? Why was she always alone in her dream house? Jim, however, didn't question a thing. He was in his own world, and he felt quite successful. He had provided Susie with the house she wanted and was still able to put a little bit into savings. He didn't notice that he often didn't see the kids until just before bedtime. He didn't realize that he had gained fifteen pounds since he had stopped going to the health club and riding his bicycle on the weekends. He didn't even think about getting his blood pressure or cholesterol checked.

Susie began asking Jim what was wrong between them and complaining that she didn't feel close to him anymore. She wanted him to be more involved with her and with the kids. She wanted him to share more of himself, especially his feelings.

Jim was aware that Susie was dissatisfied. But he knew what to do to be a better husband and father. His job was to work and make money and he was doing that quite well. So whenever Susie complained, Jim retreated to a familiar solution: he worked harder. The harder he worked, to his mind, the more successful he was. He was being a better and better husband and provider. In addition, work provided a kind of structure that reassured Jim. It was regular, predictable, and blocked his feelings of anxiety. Susie's complaints fell on ears that were deaf to her message. After all, Jim had spent so much of his life working and so little of his life learning about his feelings that he was not even going to try to get into that with her. Feelings were her territory, and he would leave them to her!

Work is a powerful form of structure for most men. It has regularity, predictability, and usually requires the man to distance himself from his feelings. When things get stressful, what better solution than to have an outlet with so much structure? It's no wonder that as the pressure built, Jim channeled more and more of his efforts into his work.

Susie and Jim have gotten into their trap together. They share some basic beliefs about their cultural roles. And although Jim's health is deteriorating, he is not yet aware that something is wrong. Susie is, and therefore she is the one who might be motivated to initiate some change. But it won't be easy for her. Her self-esteem has depended on Jim's outward success and on how that reflected on her. A part of her doesn't want him to slow down; it might mean no new furniture or clothes, or her going back to work.

Most frightening is that Jim probably won't want to change. Why mess with success? Besides, college education is right around the corner, and it's getting more and more expensive. Some of the children might want to go to a private university. His boss wants him to join the country club. He's going full speed ahead.

There are additional reasons for men to want to continue to push to earn a lot of money, including power and security. We do know that those with the money have the power in this world. They earn the big salaries, make the big deals. They get what they want; they can make choices. They can use this power for good and evil. Men have had this power throughout most of history. Why should they want to give it up?

This power is obviously used in relationships. (That is why I actually do believe that women should earn their own money.) The person who earns the money usually feels that he or she (usually he) has the final say, the veto, on how money gets spent.

Then there is the issue of security. In a funny way, it seems as though money can buy love. It can certainly buy diamonds, and they are supposed to represent love. But why is it always the men who are buying things for women? Of course, they often have more money. But I believe that there is another issue involved. Men's financial power over women leads them to feel secure. A woman's financial dependence on a man may be the only thing that allows him to feel lovable.

A personal experience drove the point home to me. On a visit out of town, my husband had an accident, fell, and broke his arm. It was his right arm, and it was splinted in one of those odd ways in which it stuck out to the side awkwardly. He was in some pain, but the largest problem was that he couldn't maneuver very well. He couldn't drive. He couldn't get dressed by himself. He couldn't cut his own food. He was helpless. He couldn't get along without me.

Suddenly, I got a new and peculiar feeling. I felt sure that he couldn't leave me *because he was dependent on me*. Now, we have a very good relationship, and I don't really think that he would leave me. But all of a sudden, I felt more secure than I had ever felt. He needed me! And even if he didn't really like me, he still couldn't leave me. What a shock this was to me. I felt powerful, important, valuable—and safe.

I think that men have a profound insecurity about their inherent lovability. After all, they have been raised to think that their value is in their actions, in what they do, not in who they are. They don't even really know why women like them. They are, after all, not really secure about their own identities. Because they often don't feel confident about their value to themselves, it is difficult to believe, deep down, that somebody else values them.

When a woman is financially dependent on a man, he has a kind of security that gives him a sense of relief. He is important; he is needed. When in doubt, he can spend money. His often unrecognized need for a woman's approval and admiration gets hidden by her financial dependence on him. She needs him, can't manage without him, and of course would not, could not, leave him. His role as provider, and therefore his maleness, is assured.

In addition, for a man, taking care of *things* is taking care of the relationship. Since he defines himself in terms of action and accomplishment, he values concrete tasks. Being a success at work, earning a good living, keeping the house safe and secure, providing the children a good education are his contributions. They are expressions of his caring, commitment, and love. But they are in a different realm and a different language from ours as women.

The emotion seems missing to us, but remember, to men, *Die Hard* is a love story.

Jim really loves Susie. He wants her to have the things that are important to her. But he isn't sure what she likes about him besides the money. So, for example, buying the children the best education possible is like buying an insurance policy on the relationship.

If Susie wants Jim to change, then, she will have to address the basic needs and insecurities that cause Jim's behavior. She will have to begin to let him know (because he apparently doesn't) what she really likes about him. Things that seem obvious to her will need to be spelled out. She will have to teach him her language and set of values. Since he has learned to value only his performance and his measurable achievements, it will be difficult for him to have much of a picture of the other dimensions of his personality. Like Steven, he has not placed emphasis on qualities like compassion, honesty, and warmth. And such things as sensitivity and vulnerability have been aspects of himself to be avoided, not cultivated.

Susie will also have to work on some of her own attitudes about work and money. Does she really want Jim to work so hard? Does her self-esteem depend on his earning power? If so, can she find other ways to feel good about herself? For her own mental health, she should develop her own abilities and self-esteem separate from how she is defined by her husband. Since she has daughters, she is almost obligated to do this in order to avoid perpetuating this cycle for them. And as long as she depends on Jim's success and actions for her own self-esteem, she will tend to be anxious about Jim's show of vulnerability, because it will throw her whole system off-balance. It will be difficult for her to support the changes she says she wants in Jim if she actually gets important emotional needs met by having Jim stay the same.

We often complain that men work too hard, and that they value their work more than they value us. They have their own reasons, which we can understand and help them with. But we have our own reasons too, and those are up to *us* to deal with.

Chapter Seven

SEX

It had been five weeks since Justin and Kay had brought their new son, Drew, home from the hospital. Drew was their first child, and they had the usual but profound adjustments that accompany becoming parents for the first time. But they'd done pretty well. They'd talked ahead of time about most of the anticipated stresses and found that their shared values kept them in tune with each other.

Kay had taken a much desired six-month leave from work. Involved though she was in her career, she wanted to spend uninterrupted time with her new child and wanted the opportunity to get adjusted to her new role as a mother. This turned out to be a good decision for her, as she was flourishing in her new life and in her new relationship with Drew.

Justin had taken some time off from work, mostly in the form of leaving early in the afternoons. He would come home and relieve Kay, and he really enjoyed that time with the baby. It was his private time, and he was feeling pretty secure that this was his child, too, not just Kay's.

But there was trouble in paradise. After a typically pleasant evening together, sharing dinner and child-care chores, Kay would take Drew to the nursery to nurse him before bedtime. Without any discussion about it, Kay seemed to assume that this was a private time for her with Drew. Drew would usually fall asleep after this feeding, and Kay would emerge from the nursery soothed and sleepy herself. She would tell Justin what a wonderful husband and father he was, tell him how much she loved him, kiss him good-night, and collapse in bed, falling into a deep sleep. There was no mention—not a hint or a clue—about Kay's having any interest in resuming her sexual relationship with Justin.

They had talked about sex as part of their planning for the new baby. The doctor had advised them that they could have intercourse after about a month, assuming Kay felt all right, and they were aware of the need for birth control despite the fact that Kay was nursing. Justin had asked about her sexual interest fairly early on. Kay explained that she felt so close to Drew during the day, especially with nursing him, that she just didn't feel any sexual desire. And since she was getting up with Drew every night, Kay was awfully tired. She figured she'd be interested in sex again, but she wasn't sure just when.

Justin felt profoundly rejected. Did Kay have no idea how this felt to him? She didn't even act as if it were a problem. Justin felt as if his role as husband was now limited to provider and father. He had impregnated her, given her this longed-for child, and now she was through with him. He was basically dispensable. She had no need for a lover, now that she had Drew. He was shocked at how insensitive she was to his needs and discouraged by her apparent refusal to even discuss the matter. Each day that Kay stayed removed from their sexual relationship, Justin emotionally withdrew from Kay just a little bit. It seemed that they each had a relationship with Drew, but not with each other. Justin felt a deep sense of loss of the relationship with Kay, anger at how left out he was, and, though he hated to admit it, jealousy of the new baby. Things weren't working out at all right.

In a scene at the beginning of the movie *Rain Man*, a man and woman are traveling together from Los Angeles to spend a weekend in Palm Springs. They've been driving for some time; the camera shows them out in the middle of the desert. As the camera takes us inside the car, we witness a dialogue that begins with her saying, "Could we have a little conversation here? Maybe you could just say ten or twelve words. . . . Consider it foreplay."

Okay, so here we are, finally talking about sex. Why did I wait so long to get to this part? For a very good reason. We want to understand how men feel about sex. But just as we can't separate our own feelings, needs, and personalities from our feelings about sex, the same is true of men. So the more we understand about their struggles, fears, needs, pressures, insecurities, values, and so on, the more we can understand their sexuality *in context.*

THE WAY TO CONNECT

For men, sex is connection. For men, sexual acceptance is necessary in order for them to feel emotional acceptance. And for men, sexual activity is a solidifying force for masculine identity.

Paul arrived home at eight o'clock after a particularly taxing day at work. His dinner was on a plate covered with plastic wrap, waiting to be reheated in the microwave. Linda was with the children, and when Paul dragged himself upstairs, he found that she was finishing up bedtime stories and that the children were almost asleep.

Linda had taken the day off from work to help her mother through cataract surgery. Linda's mother was a basically good soul, but she didn't handle helplessness very well and had been stubborn and grouchy all day long.

Paul and Linda went back downstairs; Paul mechanically ate his dinner, while Linda was at the sink, cleaning up. As Paul brought his plate to the kitchen, he got a glimpse of Linda that aroused him. Her jeans fit perfectly around her hips. And the steam from the sink was making her hair curl around her face in a most appealing way. Without a thought, Paul put down his plate, put his hand around Linda's hips, and whispered in her ear what he wanted to do.

"Don't you know what kind of day I've had today?" Linda shouted as she pulled away from him. "Save that for later."

It was three weeks later before Paul suggested it again.

Men and women live in two different worlds when it comes to sex. Women usually need an emotional connection to be interested in sex. For men, it is the other way around. Emotionally numb most of the time, for men, sex is often the only route to emotions, the only place a man may allow himself to feel.

Paul was feeling drained when he came home from work. He loved his children, and he didn't like it when he arrived home from work too late to spend time with them. He was grateful that Linda had left a plate of food out for him, but wished that he had been able to be with his family while they had dinner.

But Paul wasn't really aware of these feelings. Mostly, he just felt tired, and his mind was a blank. If he had been able to identify his feelings, he probably would have felt *lonely* and sort of left out of family life. He would have felt *sad* that he couldn't have spent more time with his children. And he might even have felt *jealous* of Linda, for having the time with the children, and of the children, for having the time with Linda.

When Paul saw Linda as so appealing, and he felt aroused, it was as if his emotional light had been turned on, not just his sexual appetite. Before he felt that sexual arousal for Linda, he had been dragging himself through the evening, feeling sort of mildly unhappy, but with no real thoughts about why. He wasn't interested in *anything*, including connecting with Linda.

Now he was alive, excited, interested, very glad that he was married to Linda. The weight that he had been feeling all evening had lifted. Life was not so bad; he felt energized and really pretty good.

When Linda rejected him, Paul was crushed. He had

permitted himself to have these feelings; he had let himself feel his need for Linda. He had been open to her. It may have been insensitive of him not to consider how she might be feeling; it may have been naive of him to think that he could just express his feeling like that and get a positive response. But his being open with her made him vulnerable to her. So when she pushed him away, and with anger and disgust, her reaction had an immediate and huge effect on him—not so much on the outside, but inside. Without even thinking, he withdrew, like a snail into his shell. He didn't come out until he felt brave enough to try to be a little open with Linda again. It would take some doing. Paul felt less open and expressive than he had before the rejection. He would be testing the waters for a while, to see if he'd get bitten again.

Now, you're probably either wondering "So, where's the sex already?" or "Is this the same old story about sex, again?" Am I trying to tell you never to say no to a man?

Well, this is about men and sex, so we are trying to understand more about men than just their penises. And, yes, you can say no to a man, but it makes a difference how you do it, and it makes a difference when you know the effect you are having. Since men use sex as a way to make an emotional connection, and since women use emotional connections as a route to sex, some serious translating is needed when it comes to sex.

THE ROUTE TO EMOTIONS

For most men, sex is the only arena in which they feel safe being openly emotional. Let's go back over what we know so far to get some clear reasons for this.

First of all, remember that men are supposed to be soldiers. They are supposed to be strong and courageous and follow orders. They have an unconscious knowledge that if there's a problem, they will have to go fix it. This kind of reality prohibits men from being very open to their emotions. If they know that they may have to give up good feelings at any moment, they will tend to keep their feelings out of their awareness.

Next, we know that men are very vulnerable to women, beginning with dependence on Mother. Women are extremely important, yet somewhat mysterious, since they live in another world. Men are never really sure how to please women. Sex is a way to get close to women, and, men hope, a way to please women.

Men tend to be structured all of the time. The structure protects them from their vulnerability. But in that state of safety, emotions don't readily get in or out. The structure is like a grid through which reality gets filtered. Everything must work a little to get through. To feel sexual pleasure with an important woman, to do more than just go through the motions, a man must let the grid down. The rest of the time, though, it's up, doing its job.

When men are in a trance, they don't feel anything. Being asked to share feelings when they are so protected is unlikely to cause them to want to break the trance. It is feelings, after all, that the trance protects them from. So pushing them to deal with feelings will push them farther back into that state. If they can be sexual, if they can really let go, it will often break the trance. Then there may be a window into their feelings.

Don't forget about social messages. The predominant message is that real men don't show their feelings. They are tough and strong. But real men *are* allowed to be sexual. In the culture of men, sex is the only arena in which some expression of feeling is acceptable. So a man can let himself be emotional when he is sexual without worrying that he is not adequate as a man. In this area, it's almost as if this show of emotion doesn't count; it's free.

And work is related to sex, too. Work is very demanding. Many of us who work outside the home have a pretty good idea about this. It is close to impossible to be an emotional person in the business or professional world. We all have our guards up. For men, this reinforces the structure. It is very difficult to make transitions, to just drop the structure, to be real and feel who you really are, when you play the game at work. Most women also have a great deal of trouble with the transition. But I think most men don't make the transition, since the emotional distance of the business world is the same as their usual emotional distance. They can very easily go to work day after day after day without shifting to a different state when they get home. Sex is one way that they can break out of that state.

The common thread that runs through these ideas, of course, is that men have a very difficult time with their feelings. They have difficulty identifying, sharing, understanding, and working with their feelings.

As Lou pulled into the garage, he was trying to decide how to tell Helen the news. This might be the worst day of his life, he thought to himself. After twenty-one years at the firm, and a recent promotion to the post of senior vice-president, he had been let go. Although the company had been having some trouble, a new marketing plan had been implemented, revenues were up, and people sounded more optimistic. Lou's layoff was a shock. He was to go to the office over the weekend to clean out his desk and credenza and was not to visit the office anymore during business hours. There would be no retirement party. He had gotten eight months' severance pay; he'd be all right for a while, but he had no future. At fifty-five, who would hire him?

He dragged himself up the stairs to the kitchen, where Helen was busy with dinner. "You're home early," she said, smiling, and ready to give him a big hug. But she pulled back when she saw his face.

"I've lost my job," Lou said simply, surprised at how the news had just come out of his mouth. He didn't look back at Helen, but walked into the den, turned on the news. When Helen tried to talk with him, he said he just wanted to be alone. He was almost silent through dinner, though he answered Helen's questions politely.

They went to bed early. Lou started nuzzling Helen, telling her how warm and wonderful she was, how good she smelled, how soft her skin was. All of a sudden he was making love to her. Now it was Helen's turn to be shocked.

How did this emotionally dead man suddenly come to life? Why was he suddenly capable of passionate love-making?

Lou is like many men who are cut off from their feelings until they become sexual. We can understand this pattern with a series of now-familiar psychological principles.

First of all, the early separation from Mother that comes with recognizing the difference from her is a shock to the boy. We all know that kind of numbness that sets in when we are traumatized. This experience sets the tone for the male's emotional life. He wants that state of closeness and oneness that he had with Mother—we all do. But he doesn't know how to get it. Vaguely but powerfully he feels the loss, with no way to repair it. He is set up to stay distant from his feelings.

Then, of course, he must repudiate all things female. This very clearly includes feelings. Boys and men are just not supposed to have them. If a man has learned that he is not supposed to have feelings, how in the world is he ever going to learn about them, including his own? The whole system, for both cultural and early developmental reasons, is set up to make men emotional illiterates. They have had no practice with their feelings. They don't know how to tell when they have one, and they don't know what to do when they have one, except make it go away. And of course they don't easily recognize them in other people, or know what to do when somebody else has one.

And then there is our dissatisfaction and impatience with men about their feelings. We probably don't realize that they are in such unfamiliar territory. We think that they are being stubborn or withholding when the answer to the question "How are you feeling?" is "Fine." But since a man has learned to ignore his feelings for his whole life, why should he know what they are? When we act frustrated, angry, or demeaning about a man's difficulty with his feelings, it does not make him want to open up! It makes him more careful than ever and even more likely to try to avoid that territory.

But in the sexual realm, the man can think of himself as competent. He has experience here. Or at least he is supposed to. Culturally, this is his territory. He doesn't have to push it away and deny its importance in the same way that he has to do with other feelings. He is freer to let himself go, to be himself, because he is not as much at risk of being seen as foolish or inadequate.

So when Lou can be sexual, he can feel good about himself, competent. What could be more important than this after being fired at age fifty-five? By expressing himself sexually, he can get the emotional closeness he needs from Helen, without getting exposed to the kind of feelings that make him feel so vulnerable. But still he is at risk. Since sex is the area in which a man is most likely to risk himself, he is actually quite vulnerable here. He lets himself go, and he makes himself open.

We may assume that because men are more comfortable in the sexual arena than in many other emotional arenas, they are confident or even fearless. And in some sense, they are confident, because they have been allowed to express themselves sexually. But in another way, they are as vulnerable as ever, for this is the one place in which they let their guard down. Since this is where they let their feelings out, they are at risk. Since this is the place where they drop the grid, the structure, they are almost defenseless. Like the snail without the shell, they are soft, and can be punctured, and very badly hurt.

Now, they won't act that way, because that is not how men act. They are more likely to act sullen or angry, or withdrawn. And since they are out of touch with their feelings, they probably don't "feel" hurt. All they feel is the defensive reaction to the injury. That defensiveness looks detached, distant, or critical. If you hurt a man sexually, don't expect him to say, "You know, honey, that really hurts my feelings and makes it difficult to be open to you." Expect him to be like Paul: gone. The more often he is hurt, the farther away he goes, making him less and less in touch with the feelings connected with sexuality and more likely to experience the sexual act as separate from a relationship.

Remember that men act in stereotypic masculine ways in order to feel more secure about their masculinity. There is no reason to think that this is any different in the sexual realm than in other areas. And when it comes to sexuality, since men tend to let themselves be more exposed, they also have to be more protective. They don't feel confident just because they act confident. They actually bruise easily.

So if your man isn't pleasing you, be aware of how you tell him. If you give him lots of instructions right when he is letting himself go, he'll feel like he has failed. He'll either lose his erection or he'll lose his emotion. This doesn't mean that you shouldn't tell him what you would like him to do to please you. It *does* mean that you should be prepared for the effects that you cause. Though many men would like to think that when it comes to sex, they are skilled and relaxed, remember that if they let themselves have feelings with you, they are just as vulnerable as you are. Perhaps they are more vulnerable, because if they are the more active partner in sex, they are showing even more.

BIOLOGY—THE POWER OF THE PENIS

One last time, we are going back to thinking about that little boy. Before he is a year old, he has discovered his penis.

A baby develops from top to bottom. His nervous system is immature, and the order in which it starts to get active generally goes from head to toe. So you see a baby put everything in his mouth. Then he becomes fascinated by his hands. Eventually, he finds his feet, and he has a great time when he realizes that those feet belong to him!

The baby is not the first one to find these parts of his body, of course. His parent is. Usually the mother has been bathing and changing and caressing him. When she changes his diaper, the mother washes off his penis. As that part of the nervous system becomes more and more developed, this begins to feel pretty good to the baby. When he finds that he can reach down and grab his penis himself, he is thrilled. He smiles and laughs as he enjoys the physical sensation.

Obviously, there are some differences for the baby girl.

Although she too experiences genital sensations, her genitals are not so readily accessible. The mother washes her genitals differently than she does her son's. It would be impossible for the experience to be the same for the girl as for the boy. The baby girl does stimulate herself genitally, when she finds the source of pleasure, but it's usually not with the same kind of unabashed delight.

It is difficult to separate the biological factors from the social factors, because a particular piece of our culture comes into play as this physical development takes place. We live in what can be termed a "phallocentric" society. ("Phallus" is Greek for "penis.") Literally, this means a society that focuses on the penis. What it actually means, though, is that our society is focused on those who *possess* a penis.

So it's pretty common for the family to make something of a fuss about the baby boy's marvelous discovery. Or they think it's cute. And they give this part of him a name. (Many girls don't know the name of their genitals until they reach adolescence.) So the baby boy has a part of himself that is easily accessible, that feels absolutely marvelous to touch, that can soothe him when he is feeling badly, and that everyone else seems to love, too. His penis has become a very important part of himself.

This focus on the penis doesn't stop as the boy grows up. Little boys talk about their penises all the time. As they get a little older, they talk about their penises with each other. They compare how their penises look, and, of course, how big they are. When they learn how to masturbate, they talk about it, and they often do it together. Size and speed and prowess get to be important. As they reach adolescence and huge amounts of hormones begin to have their effects, masturbation, pictures of nude women, and thinking and talking about erections, hard-ons, and having sex become close to obsessional.

Our culture supports this. We still have a double standard, in which a boy is supposed to get a little experience and sow a few wild oats. No one really wants to think about whose field they get sowed in. It's certainly not supposed to be with his female classmates. But it is supposed to happen. It's a part of his growing up. So no wonder the boy continues to focus on and feel good about his penis. Everybody else seems to. (As a society, we're in big trouble now, because of the AIDS epidemic. This sexual experimentation is not so cute anymore, but it is very difficult to stop.)

As we have said earlier, the boy's masculine identity is tenuous. How could there be a better way of reassuring himself of his masculinity than to be sexually secure? What he can do, no woman can do. He can ejaculate, and how exhilarating that is! If he performs as a man, he clearly distinguishes himself as not-woman. If he measures up sexually, he measures up as a man.

We also know that the approval of other men is vital to a man's confidence in his masculinity. So if other men approve of his sexual ability, he again measures up. He wants to look good, strong, and confident, and the temptation to exaggerate is powerful. Men embellish their reports of performance in areas of power such as sports, investments, salary. One very successful millionaire pointed out that 98 percent of investment stories are about men's successes, but men rarely talk of their failures. So I know that all men don't actually tell the truth to each other about sex! I am reminded of the scene from the movie *When Harry Met Sally*, when Harry claims he always satisfies women in bed and Sally questions that claim. She points out that men *always* say that they're good lovers, and women *always* say that they sometimes fake orgasm. But to the man, the fiction is as important as the reality. This aspect of men's masculine identity is another factor in the man's focusing on his sexual ability and experience, another aspect of the social focus on the man's penis.

Biology has a role to play here, too, and sometimes sex is purely biological, detached from connection or relationships. Often, then, men get involved with prostitutes or in affairs, without any sense, in their own minds, that this reflects badly on the woman they are with or on the relationship. As difficult as it is for us to believe, when a man says about an affair, "It has nothing to do with you," he can really mean it.

Though for most women, sexual involvement implies that a real relationship is possible, for most men, such an implication is not automatic. For many men, it is important and quite possible to be able to have sex for its own sake, without the problems and entanglements of relationships. Sometimes what a man wants is to copulate with a woman's body. Who she is, or that she is a person at all, is irrelevant. She doesn't have to have an identity—she can be asleep or drunk. As the World War II expression goes, "Throw a flag over her face and do it for Old Glory."

Remember, too, that the route to relationship is different for men and women. Men do get relationally involved through sex. There's a saying that goes "Women will do anything for love, even sex. Men will do anything for sex, even love," and there's something real in this. Sometimes it's after the sex that the man feels the connection. In the scene from *Rain Man*, the woman wants the man to talk. She needs that kind of connection in order to feel comfortable having sex later on. ("Consider it foreplay.") The man, meanwhile, doesn't need or want to feel emotional while driving through the desert. But he'll be ready for sex when they get to the hotel room.

The differences between men's sexual relationships and women's can be especially difficult and painful for single women. After the first night together, a man says good-bye to a woman and adds, "I'll call you." But he never does. Why not? Two reasons stand out. Sometimes, for a man, the sex has no relational part to it at all. He never means to call; he's just saying what is expected at the time. Can you imagine his saying, "So long. The sex was pretty good, but don't expect to see me or hear from me again"? Honest, perhaps, but poor form.

Sometimes, the man is actually interested in the woman. But he has made himself vulnerable, and he is frightened of this. Most of the time, I do not think that the man is aware of the vulnerability. But he experiences a need to get distance from the woman, rather than a need to get closer. This is especially confusing for the woman in this case, because she has been accurate in her perception that she and her date were getting along very well and enjoying each other. But often this feeling, which naturally makes her want to spend more time together and entertain thoughts of the future, makes him want to get away and stay away.

This is a sad situation, and there are few things a woman can do about it. She has to remember that for her, the sexual involvement brings a feeling of closeness and a sense of the relationship's being more solid. She feels safer. But for the man, the sexual involvement, if it suggests more closeness, means danger. What this means is that if a woman is wanting to develop a relationship with a man, she should be thoughtful about how soon she gets sexually involved. Since sex opens him up so much more, he has more of a chance of feeling safe if he has a wider base in the relationship.

If a woman wants to have sex right away with a man, she may want to decide that, for her, it is acceptable that this be a purely sexual encounter. Often the man's need to put distance between them is overpowering to him, and his response to this is automatic. Most of the time, the only thing a woman can do is to work hard not to personalize the rejection. It may be little comfort, but it's better than always blaming the failure of the relationship on one's own inadequacies.

SEX IN RELATIONSHIPS

Once in a relationship, the man needs acceptance and reassurance for what is important about him to himself. (We are all made that way.) His sexuality has become very important to him. Sexual acceptance is crucial for him to be able to experience emotional acceptance, and sexual rejection can mean rejection of his whole self. He is not very likely to distinguish between the two.

Kay's rejection of Justin is very much like that. She doesn't even realize that she is rejecting him. Sex has such a different meaning for her at this point that she is oblivious to his sensitivity. He, on the other hand, has so much personal validation attached to Kay's sexual involvement with him that he is also unaware of the profound adjustment she is going through. He just thinks she loves Drew more, and loves him less, if at all.

Kay assumes that Justin understands how she feels, and that her lack of interest in sex has nothing to do with her feelings for Justin. She is, of course, wrong, and she reached her erroneous conclusion by using only her own frame of reference. Justin assumes that Kay doesn't care about him, that she knows how important it would be to him to be sexually involved, but chooses not to meet his need. He, too, reaches his false conclusion based on his perspective alone. The first step for them to take in resolving their difficulty is to talk to each other about their individual needs and motivations. Only then can they each decide what they can do differently.

Sexual activity is a solidifying force for male identity. So for a man, refusal can mean loss of his sense of himself as well as loss of love. By this I do *not* mean that men should be able to have sex with anyone any time they want it because otherwise they'll feel bad! I mean that in a committed relationship, these factors come into play.

It's finally time to get back to Linda and Paul. It isn't that Linda should drop the dishes, close the kitchen door, and make love with Paul right on the spot because he's ready to be emotionally close to her and she shouldn't hurt his feelings or pass up this opportunity. But if she wants to be connected to him, she'll want to encourage his form of expressing closeness.

Linda will be a lot more comfortable with Paul if she tries to translate his communication for herself. "You make me feel as steamy as those dishes" does not translate into "You're a wonderful person and I want to be close to you." It *is* about sex. It does translate into "I'm excited about you." That's not a bad thing to hear after the day that Linda has had, in which she feels that she has given to everyone else and isn't much appreciated. If she hears Paul's suggestion as his involvement with her, she could respond positively, let Paul know that she loves him, and then she could say that she'd just like to finish up and she'll be with him. Then she can think. What does she want?

The closeness of sex might be quite a relief for her. But if she is too angry, and doesn't have the energy for it, she could say, "I'm glad you feel that way, honey. But I've had such a bad day, and I feel so angry, that I don't think I'd be very pleasant tonight. Could we just cuddle and be close a little bit? I'm sure I'll feel better tomorrow."

Paul might be disappointed and even a little hurt. But he probably won't need to withdraw as much. He might, then, be available to Linda for what she needs: a little ventilation about her day and her mother and *her* disappointment about the family's not being together that evening.

If Paul and Linda can work this out, they will probably both feel that they are making compromises. "I'll do this for her," he'll think, or she'll think, "I'll do this because it's important to him." (As if that's such a bad thing.) Over time, they will learn from each other. Linda will realize that it feels good to make Paul feel good, even if having sex wasn't what she thought she wanted to do just then. She might even enjoy it herself. And Paul will learn that when Linda says that she isn't interested in sex, it doesn't mean that she isn't interested in him. When he really learns that, he will be on his way to expanding his emotional repertoire, and to learning that there are lots of ways in addition to sex that he might be able to use to feel good with Linda.

Chapter Eight

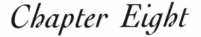

"NUMEROLOGY"

Picture this: You have just been seated at the local arena for a concert by your favorite pop artist. Getting there has been a harrowing experience. The traffic has been re-routed because of the crowds, so the parking was confusing. Luckily, you arrived early, because it was about a half-mile walk from where the traffic cop had made you park. You walk around to the other side of the stadium to find your seats. You climb over eight people to get there.

But you are excited. As you pull your coat off and arrange yourself, you are surveying the scene and the crowd. The stage is huge, and you can't wait to see the special effects and costumes. The performance has gotten rave reviews in other cities, and you are really glad you were lucky enough to get tickets.

The arena is pretty full and a little bit noisy. People keep milling about the way they do. You wish the show would start. You're excited. You turn to your husband and put your arm around his shoulder.

"Isn't this great? I am so excited. It's so much fun to be here with you. It was kind of a hassle getting here, but now that we're here, it feels like it was worth it."

"Yeah. You know, there are about eighteen thousand seats here, not counting that orange section behind the stage that's empty. There are still about forty-five hundred empty seats and the concert is supposed to start in ten minutes. They can't be seating more than one hundred and fifty people a minute. So I figure that this is going to start at least a half hour late. I think I'll go get a hot dog and a beer. Do you want something, honey?"

Is this a conversation? Who *cares* how many seats there are? It's great to be together. Sure, it's a big place, and there are a lot of people here. Why is he always counting?

I'll tell you why I think he is always counting. Frankly, it wasn't easy to get to this concert. This isn't a familiar environment, so he doesn't know what's going to happen. He is not in charge. He is not in control. He must do something to counteract his anxiety and disorientation. His counting acts as a tranquilizer. (She might fluff her hair, he counts seats.) It makes him less frightened and unsure. It turns the unfamiliar into the familiar.

Ah, men and their numbers. There are countless (pardon the pun) stories!

Phil's got a tape measure clipped to his belt. He's wearing a pager with digital memory—of course. There's a compass glued to the dashboard of his car, a radar detector on the visor, and a tire gauge, among other measuring devices, in the glove compartment. He has road maps from all his vacations in the trunk and two city maps in the glove compartment. He keeps a small book with his gasoline purchases and a running account of current miles per gallon; he's always setting his trip odometer, even when he's just buzzing around town.

A schedule of the season's football games hangs by his bed with the scores written in from the games so far. Next to each game is the name of the person in the office who won that week's pool. Phil knows the top college players and keeps an updated log of the order of picks he is predicting for next year's NFL draft.

Julie was tired of going to Jim's mother's for Christmas every year. But she didn't know if Jim would agree to go to her sister's. She knew Jim pretty well, though, and so she knew how to find out how he would feel about it.

"On a scale of one to ten, with one being 'you couldn't stand it' and ten being 'nothing would please you more,' how would you feel about going to my sister's this year for Christmas?" asked Julie.

"About a six," said Jim.

Elaine and Frank have been married for twenty years but have just started to try understanding instead of being disappointed in each other. Elaine has been feeling very badly about Frank's not following through with a business deal that would help them out financially and give Elaine a sense of security. She has been telling him that she has been feeling very distressed about this for three years, but he hasn't taken any action.

One day, Frank tells Elaine about his partner's distress dealing with his wife's third miscarriage. His partner is suffering a great deal. Elaine says, "Frank, do you realize that I feel as badly about this business deal as your partner does about his wife?"

"You do?"

Frank finally acts. In couples' counseling, Elaine asks Frank what was different—why did he finally seem to understand that she really felt very badly?

Frank was able to explain that he had been feeling upset about the business deal, too. So when Elaine said she felt badly, Frank figured she felt badly the way he did (which was not great, but not terrible). It wasn't until Elaine said she felt as bad as his partner that he understood.

He explained, "You never quantified it before."

Maybe it's brain structure or chemistry. Maybe it's because the left side of the brain is overdeveloped in men. Maybe it's the result of a high level of testosterone circulating in the bloodstream.

There are scientific studies demonstrating the concrete reality that men's brains are different from women's. Men's brains are shown to operate differently than women's do, with greater visual-spatial abilities. And studies also show that the actual structure of men's and women's brains are different, with men's brains showing more development in the left hemisphere, the part of the brain that specializes in rational, logical thinking.

It's hardly a newsbreaking "discovery" that men think differently than we do. The studies show real differences between men and women. However, the reasons for these differences are not that clear. Some suggest that a man just thinks the way nature intended him to think. It's all biological. If we look at our biological history, men have probably needed to be able to protect their pregnant women, fight off invaders, and kill sabertooth tigers. The biological necessity may well be reflected in the way a man thinks and processes information. There isn't any need for an explanation of how he learned to think this way. He just does.

I don't agree with this. I think it's more complicated and more interesting than that. The way I see it is that in addition to their natural biological endowment, men *learn* to think this way. And I think that *numbers* help men handle their fears, worries, insecurity, and uncertainty.

Men keep score. Everything is measured, enumerated, coded, graded, and compared. Remember that men have been accustomed to using structure to make themselves comfortable. The language of feelings is unfamiliar and confusing to them, a vast, strange, unmarked territory, filled with inconsistency and danger. But numbers are dependable and safe. A man can orient himself through numbers; they can help him find a familiar place. When he's unsure, he counts. He *knows*, he is secure, when he can count.

Here is one of my favorite personal examples. When my husband and I meet at home after work, I always want to know how his day was. I want to know what kind of mood he is in as we prepare to spend the evening together. I want to know whether he feels good about his work. I want to know if there were any particular difficulties or successes. In addition to having a pretty full caseload of patients, he teaches psychiatric residents, meets many interesting clinicians for lunches, is training director of a psychoanalytic institute, and is on the board of directors of a small but exciting engineering firm. It's pretty interesting. Invariably, this is how he answers my question "How was your day?":

"Let's see. Seven-fifteen—good, very good. Eight o'clock—really good. Eight-forty-five—excellent, we made a real breakthrough today. Ten o'clock—okay. Could have been better. Well, actually, that was pretty good. Ten forty-five—quite difficult, but really productive. Eleven-thirty—good, very good . . ."

This goes on and on until the whole day is accounted for. Does it mean anything to me? Very little. I don't know who these people are. I don't know what they are working on together. I don't know if this "breakthrough" was six weeks or six years in the making. I don't know how he *feels* about his day.

I've told him about this. He can't do it any other way. He is actually trying to answer me. He knows that I would not be satisfied if he said what he would more automatically say: "Fine" or "Not too bad." He knows that I want to know what his day was like, but he doesn't have a global impression until he has mapped out the details. Then it starts to come back to him. And I can ask specific questions about what sounds interesting. (Although what can you say about "seven-fifteen—very good"?)

This procedure is uncomfortable for me. It makes me nervous when he counts through his day. But it is what makes sense to him. It makes him feel comfortable. He is secure with it. It keeps him from being ruled by his feelings. And, very importantly, it orients him, it locates him.

But it is always difficult to believe that something that makes you feel so frustrated can make someone else feel so good.

This is a lot like blowing your nose in China. You remember, saving the mucus in a piece of paper in your pocket versus blowing it out on the sidewalk in front of you. If I try to think about what I must sound like to my husband when I'm telling him about *my* day, I imagine it must sound something like this:

"Boy, am I hungry. This was a very long day. A good day, but a long day . . . Let me get something to drink first before I tell you the details. And a snack . . . Do you want to cook something here or should we go out? Because if we're going to go out, I'd like to go right away. Then I can tell you about what this day was like.

"Oh, and you won't *believe* what happened at St. Vincent's today. I was *so* mad! You know that presentation we were supposed to make about our research project, the presentation they wanted us to make with less than a month's notice last summer, that they rescheduled for the spring? The one Sandra and I have done all that work preparing? Well, they scheduled someone else for that time slot. Someone from outside the hospital, so they're canceling *us*! Can you *believe* it? I am *so* mad.

"So, do you want to eat out?"

You can't say that my description of my day is any clearer than my husband's description of his day! It must make his head spin. How could he listen to this? He must be trying to hang in there to figure out what's going on. I think I am expressing myself. I am sharing my feelings.

I am telling him what is important, giving him a general impression of how my day was for me. That's what I want him to know. I want him to know how I *feel*. Do you think he has any idea of what is going on?

What makes me comfortable is to "let it all hang out," to sort of get things out of my system. I want to share my successes and frustrations—they feel more real that way. What makes him comfortable is to stay organized, orderly, coherent, and on track. He does not want to be swayed by the feeling of the moment. He's used to feeling in control. Numbers help him do this. And they do this effectively and powerfully. They work!

THERE IS SAFETY IN NUMBERS

There is something perfect about calling this process "numerology." I think this term captures the essence of the *magic* of numbers. (Actually, numerology is defined as the study of the occult significance of numbers.) Men live by the magic of numbers—they gain nourishment as well as a sense of security and well-being from them. They feel powerful. They belong. They *know*. Pat Conroy used the word "numerology" in this particular way in his novel *The Prince of Tides*. In this passage, Tom is speaking of his father, a shrimper:

> He made his three children memorize at an early age the essential numbers of his boat before he would confer official status on us as members of the crew. Shrimp-

ing always involves a tireless worship of numerology and when shrimpers discuss their boats they toss arcane figures back and forth that define the capabilities of their respective crafts. My father's main engine was a 6-DAMR-844 Buda manufactured by the Allis-Chalmers Company, Boston. It developed 188 horse-power at 2100 rpm. His reduction gear was a 3.88.1 Capitol. The brass shaft turned a 44-by-36-inch four-blade Federal propeller. The main bilge pump was a 1¼-inch Jabsco. In the deck-house was a 42-inch Marty's wheel, a Ritchie compass, a Marmac throttle and clutch controls, and a Metal Marine automatic pilot. There was a Bendix DR16 depth recorder and a Pearce Simpson Atlantic 70 radio. On deck, the Miss Lila carried a Stroudsburg 515½ T-hoist. . . . For me this language was as *comforting as mother's milk* [italics mine] and served as the background music of the part of childhood spent afloat. . . . It all meant that my father's boat, if properly handled, could catch one hell of a lot of shrimp.

To me, this passage is wonderful because it captures not only the structuring function of numbers, but the soothing, nurturing quality of them. As you get a feeling for the secure world this was for the shrimpers, you also get a feeling for how the numbers connect the men and initiate them into a private club. It helps us see through to the feelings behind the numbers.

It's the middle of the night. I wake up, aware that the light is on.

"Are you all right?" I ask.

"Yeah, I was just thinking."

Thinking isn't what I would do in the middle of the night. "Can't you sleep?" I ask.

"No, I've been up for a while. I've been going over what I owe on that property in my pension fund and how quickly I might be able to pay off that debt. Considering the interest rate on the mortgage and the current interest rate, I'm figuring out whether I'll save money by paying it off early or if I'd do better by keeping it in zero coupons."

"Are you going to be able to go to sleep soon?"

"Yeah, as soon as I finish this."

And he will go to sleep. He'll feel better after he's done his calculations. He is comforted by the concreteness, the solidity of the numbers. It seems that it hardly matters how bad the numbers might be, just as long as he figures them out and has them. Then he has a structure, a framework, a certainty, something to hold onto. The tension is relieved and he can go back to sleep.

As we recall from chapter 3, structure is the means of providing safety in the threatening world of feelings and relationships. Structure is the general description of this process, of this tendency to put things in a concrete framework. Numbers are the ultimate structure. With numbers, you know *exactly* where you are. If you can perform some calculations, then you can know exactly where the other person is. Then you can know the status of the relationship. What a relief!

If you add up how much money you have now (including having no money) with how much money you will have in the future, you get a number. That number is something you can hang onto—it becomes a part of your reality. When my husband is thinking about how much money is in his retirement plan, he is worried about whether there is enough. He can come up with a number that is enough. It does not matter that that number does not represent the current reality. Once it is stated and is concrete, it is reality. It is soothing and reassuring.

I actually think this sounds pretty great. Oh, that it were that simple for me to reassure myself! It's a lot more complicated for me. I think I would actually have to *have* the money, not merely the counting of the money, to be reassured.

Sharon and Tim have a long, satisfying marriage with a single running conflict: no matter where they are, no matter what they are doing or talking about, when it's twenty-two minutes after the hour, Tim wants to listen to the financial report on the radio.

"Do you have to listen to that *every* time?" asks Sharon.

"It's only for two minutes."

"But those are two very important minutes. It makes me feel like I'm not very important. Those numbers are more important than I am."

"But it's only two minutes."

Numbers are like a narcotic, a fix. And Tim has to have his fix several times a day. He can't miss it without feeling undone. When he has heard his report, he has his equilibrium, and he feels good. It's so important and it feels so good that even in a relationship as good as the one that Tim has with Sharon, he can't really hear her complaint.

It's "mother's milk" that the numbers are for him, and he cannot do without it.

And men have been deprived of that mothering. They had to be big boys when they were still quite little. They have developed comforting structures, like rituals, to soothe the need for, to substitute for, security. Their need for security continues in a painful way that is hidden from all of us. All we see are the indirect manifestations of it. Obsession with numbers is one of these manifestations.

THE SECRET CODE

"That was his third triple double."

"The Dow Jones Industrial Average is 2832.58."

"The engine develops 352 horsepower @3800 rpm and has a 3.2 overhead cam."

"The barometer is 29.9 and rising; the temperature is 26 degrees and the wind chill is –5 degrees."

If you've been initiated into the club, then you know what these things mean. While we girls were learning how to prepare a tea party, the boys were playing with their Jack Armstrong secret decoder rings. While we were playing school, they were playing submarine, measuring the depth and firing fore torpedoes one and two and turning right full rudder. While we were cutting out paper dolls, they were keeping track of their favorite baseball players, with all their batting averages memorized (meaning, of course, AB's, RBI's, HR, and slugging percentages).

They belonged by knowing these numbers. They understood what was important, what was valued, and they could share it with each other in complete clarity and certainty with numbers. They learned the code and then they were included. And they were secure. As long as they knew the numbers.

It's like a secret language. When you know the language, then you are a member of the club. Like the hardware store club. If you can talk hardware, you belong. Since men have difficulty feeling connected on an emotional level, numbers provide a wonderfully structured way to have this connection. And since men are always in need of concrete proofs of their masculinity (the club to which they most need to belong), they can use their knowledge of numbers to reassure themselves and prove to others that they do indeed belong.

As I try to think of examples of this, I keep coming up blank, but that's because I'm stuck with my own experience. I think of my brother playing sports or in the Boy Scouts. I know they were talking numbers, but I don't know what they were. My husband could tell me some, but he's not home. I comb my bookshelves, which contain lots of novels and philosophy, but nothing on numbers, so I turn to something written about sports or business.

Here's an example. This is from George Will's book about baseball, *Men at Work*:

On August 13, 1910, there was a baseball game of perfect symmetry. The Pirates and Dodgers played to an 8-8 tie. Each team had 38 at bats. Each had 13 hits. Each had 12

assists. Each had 5 strikeouts, 3 walks, 2 errors, 1 bats-
man and 1 passed ball.

But that's not from my head; it's from a book.

I wait till my husband gets home. I ask for examples.
He says this stuff is fun, because you're connecting with
somebody. If I think about the exciting part of something
being about numbers, I ought to be able to come up with
some ideas. For example:

You meet somebody at a gas station, traveling.

"How many miles per gallon do you get with that
model?"

"I've been averaging twenty-six in the city and thirty-
seven or thirty-eight on the highway."

"Really? What kind of engine is it—how many cylin-
ders?"

"It's a standard V-6. I have gotten forty-one miles on
the highway with super unleaded. But that's fifteen cents
more per gallon. So I figure it isn't worth it."

"I know what you mean. Some people say it's better
for your engine, but if it costs fifteen percent more in
price but only gets you ten percent better mileage,
what's the point?"

Or, here's another one. You're talking with someone
who's taking a mountain bicycle tour:

"So you're going to do Ride the Rockies. What's that
like?"

"Well, it's three hundred seventy-seven miles in five days. That's an average of seventy-five miles a day."

"What's the elevation gain?"

"We go over only two major passes, but there is an average of six thousand feet per day in elevation gain."

"So you ride for eight hours a day. Are there time-keepers during the race?"

"Oh, yes. There are checkpoints every five miles giving you total miles, miles that particular date, and miles per hour that day."

"That's great. Maybe I'll do it next year!"

I know for myself that I would never start a conversation with a stranger about gas mileage. If someone asked me about my car's gas mileage, I would say it was pretty good or pretty bad and I would have one number that I learned when I first got the car. When I talk with someone about Ride the Rockies, it's usually commenting about how I've heard that it's something that you're glad that you did once so that you never have to do it again!

But I do know how to calculate gas mileage. And, having driven back and forth across the country every chance I got when I was in college, I also am good at reading maps. So when my husband and I travel by car, I participate in the counting of total miles, cost of gasoline, estimated time of arrival, total time of the trip, total miles traveled, and minutes till we get to the town where we'll stop for dinner. He tells me that it is so wonderful for him that I'm his partner in this that it is like a gift. He compares it to his sending me flowers. I have to believe him because he wouldn't make that up. But I have to take it on faith; it is so different from my own experience that it is almost impossible to connect with the feeling. I know, though, that it is true.

Believing this even though we don't feel it is what is critical in learning to understand each other. Accepting that his experience is truly different from yours will make a lot of his behavior make sense. And if it pleases him when you calculate the ETA, why not do it? He probably brings you flowers because he knows it makes you feel good, not because he enjoys walking into the florist's shop and choosing between chrysanthemums and carnations.

He feels safe with numbers, he feels connected, and he feels that he belongs. He feels soothed, nourished, and protected by numbers. He learns this as he is learning masculine culture, as he is learning to handle the traumas and losses of his position and role in life. And he has a biological predisposition to organize his thinking this way.

Numbers are so absorbing that they are a perfect way to enter or to stay in the trance. And they are so exact and predictable that they provide the kind of structure that is the basis of so much of men's psychological functioning. And they are a common language, providing a secure kinship with other men.

So now at least you know what you are working with. There are times that you must ask him to stop, when you really need something different from him. If Sharon needs to share something really important with Tim, such as that she is thinking of returning to work after twenty years, or that a friend has just been diagnosed with cancer, he should wait until twenty-two minutes after the *next* hour for his financial report.

How does Sharon get Tim to understand how important this issue is to her? After all, it isn't only in crises that this disruption hurts her, but it hurts her all the time. Generally, of course, she will try to tell him that his behavior hurts and angers her. But from his perspective, there is no reason why it should. Why should the soothing of "mother's milk" ever disturb anyone? Sharon is going to have to show Tim that for her to listen to the financial news while they are talking together is as painful for her as *not* listening to the financial news is to him. Knowing what this means to him is the only way to be able to make this comparison.

There are plenty of times, though, when just understanding him will make all the difference in the world. When we don't take them personally, differences can be interesting, funny, and a source of shared humor. And sometimes (try it!), it's even fun to just give in and calculate the MPG and ETA.

Chapter Nine

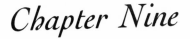

SPORTS

"And now, the statistics!"

"This is only the second time in National League history that a left-handed rookie has batted more than .300 in the play-offs."

"In last week's game, Houston completed only two of eleven third-down attempts. That's the biggest reason why they lost the game. They couldn't convert their third-down opportunities."

"Only a truly outstanding megastar like Magic Johnson, Michael Jordon, Hakeem, and a few others could score a quadruple double. Great players may do a triple double, but only the truly great can do a quadruple double."

"Four hundred yards in one game! This is only the third time this season that any quarterback has done it."

What are they talking about?

"I guess I just don't think every birthday should be that important to me," said Cindy, as she watched the waitress pour her another cup of coffee. She was having lunch with her two best friends, wishing they could help her stop feeling so bad. "If John wants to take Stu to tennis camp, why should I try to stop him?"

"But couldn't they just go the next week? Then they'd be here for your birthday. You wouldn't miss either of *their* birthdays, would you?" pushed her friend Jeannie.

"Of course not. But you don't know how important this tennis thing is to John. He thinks Stu could be a world-class tennis player. I don't know how anyone can say that about a nine-year-old boy. But that's the way John is. This sports thing is the biggest thing in his life. And he says that they have to go this particular week because the teacher that will be there will be the best to help Stu work on his serve."

"I know how bad you must feel about your birthday," said Julie. "And I know how hopeless it seems. In my house, the 'big' game takes precedence over everything. I've given up fighting it. So let's just all go out for a fancy dinner on your birthday. We'll celebrate with you!"

How can John be so insensitive?

Sherry understood that Ron didn't really have much interest in being involved in the wedding plans. He cared about who his best man was, and he wanted there to be plenty of champagne. But other than those things, anything Sherry set up was fine with him. She was hoping, though, that he'd have more interest in planning the honeymoon.

"I'd like to go some place where we can swim and relax. I don't want to travel around and sight-see. I think we'll be too tired, and we'll just want to wind down."

Ron agreed. They agreed on Hawaii as the best choice. As they were picking a hotel, Ron focused on the golf courses at or near each hotel. Some of the hotels even offered special packages, with at least one round of golf or tennis a day included in the price. Since Sherry didn't play golf, Ron figured that she could play tennis while he played golf. As they were comparing prices at the different resorts, Ron explained to Sherry what a good deal they could get on the golf.

"You're going to spend our honeymoon playing golf!" shrieked Sherry. "A honeymoon is a time to be together."

"But we will be together," insisted Ron. "We'll have breakfast together every morning. Then you can sit and read by the pool. You love to do that. Or you could play tennis while I play golf. Then we can meet for lunch. Then we'll have dinner together every evening. We can even go dancing. The big hotels all have discos and some of them have live bands. We'll be together every day."

Sherry was panicked, and even thought about calling off the wedding. Golf every day! If this was what Ron thought about the honeymoon, what would the rest of the marriage be like? she wondered.

Alice actually likes to watch sports on TV, and so do the kids. One game at a time, that is. That's why they always leave Roy alone when he's got himself positioned in front of the TV on a weekend afternoon. He watches *all* the games.

It seems as if he cannot stand to miss a crucial play in any of the games. He also catches up on the status of the games that are not being broadcast in his area. Plus the commentaries on each channel about today's games, as well as the significance of each game in the overall picture of the season. He's quite expert at timing all of this by now and wields the remote control with the skill and finesse of a champion Nintendo player.

Roy is so devoted to sports on TV that he won't let anything interfere, including the ordinary requirements of life. And he doesn't want his TV watching to be disrupted by Alice's requests that he do things or her complaints that he doesn't. So he will typically get up at the crack of dawn on Saturday, get the lawn mowed, the car washed, the dog shampooed, and the bills paid, so there will be no grounds for interference in his chosen "activity."

Alice and the kids just figure that they're on their own on the weekends. Now that they have cable, the sports coverage lasts way into the night, and so does Roy's passionate involvement. When Roy "returns" the next day, he seems in good spirits and ready to rejoin the family. So nobody fights it anymore.

But does it just have to be a cease-fire?

Sports may leave us cold, but for men, there is nothing like them. Nothing. For men, sports have everything. They meet all of men's needs. I used to think that they met all of men's needs except sex, until it was pointed out to me that they probably meet that need too. And I think that's true.

No wonder men are so involved with sports. I don't think there is anything in women's lives to compare with this involvement. There is no single outlet or focus that is as consuming and satisfying as sports can be for men, although we can find some similarities in the area of child care. In caring for an infant, a mother's attention is drawn away from everything else; nursing an infant is something a woman may do to the exclusion of anything else. By getting in touch with these feelings, we can get an idea of the degree of importance that sports have for men. But though these things may be as compelling, they do not meet such a broad range of needs as sports do for men.

So here we are complaining about sports, wondering why they spend so much time on them, feeling neglected and unimportant in comparison. But sports handle everything (including problems, confusions, and conflicts caused by us). Why would men give them up? In fact, the more we complain about and criticize them for sports, the tighter they hang on.

The more I know about sports, the easier for me to take my husband's fascination with them. Besides, when I know about them, I actually find some parts interesting. Or at least I find men's interest in them interesting! So I'm going to go back through what we've already learned and look at how many problems sports solves, how many areas they cover, how perfect they are.

NOTHING DOES IT LIKE SPORTS

For starters, we have the metaphor of the soldier. Well, sports are like war. There is often a symbolic battle, with a team and a leader. When you root for a team, you think of them as fighting your battle. If you get really involved and identify with your team, then, in a way, you are fighting the battle, too.

In sports, there are special rivalries that go on year after year. There is intense competition, as if to the death. There are strategies, and there are plans. There are flags and trophies for the victors. It's like fighting a battle, but a safe one, one with toy soldiers. Usually, no one dies, as hard as they fight. There is a clear winner and loser. It is definite and final.

How many times have we heard the TV theme, "The thrill of victory, the agony of defeat"? When his team wins, a man is on top of the world; when it loses, he can get really depressed. (In fact, whole cities can become depressed or euphoric, with parades and media attention worthy of returning war heroes.) These wins and losses are as if they were his own, because sports are most rewarding when he is immersed in them, really involved. They can also be a distraction for a man who is avoiding his own emotional issues.

In sports, the team is everything. Loyalty to the team is rule number one. It carries on that military spirit. And the team always gets the credit. The individual is always modest. The other team is always respected. That's how it's done. If you watch an interview with a winning player, he'll say things like, "I'm just one player," or "I couldn't have done this without the team," or "I owe it all to my coach," and, of course, "They played a great game. We just got all the breaks today." You never brag about your own abilities. There is a wonderful scene in *Bull Durham* in which Nuke, the rookie ball player, is being coached by Crash, the veteran, in these niceties—what to say, what not to say, and how to say it. Watch that scene, and then watch the sports news. It's enlightening. (Muhammad Ali is one of the few sports figures who tooted his own horn. Of course, boxers don't have as much of a team.)

Structure is the sense of regulation and order that keeps men psychologically safe. In sports, rules and structures abound. The game is nothing without its rules. And they keep making up more rules, year after year. The games get more complicated, and to men, that makes them more interesting, and more helpful, psychologically. In a professional football game, for example, there are under ten minutes of real physical contest, and sixty minutes of actual game time. But the event actually takes about three hours. Those time-outs get longer and longer because there are more rules to take into account, new interpretations of the rules, instant replays, commentaries on the replays, commentaries on the rules, on interpreting the rules, on the different referees. It goes on and on. It's what makes sports so compelling for men. They can get totally absorbed in the rules and the game.

Part of the reason the games are sometimes a little tedious for us is that we don't know enough of the rules. To us, it all looks like some guys are trying to move a ball back and forth across a field or a court. But that is only a small part of it. What matters is who is allowed to move it, from where to where, for how long, by what method, until what happens, and in what outstanding manner some men are doing it. It also matters who has done it before, and if it was the longest, fastest, most often, or least often. That's what they're paying attention to. They feel secure when they can tabulate and categorize it all.

A man absorbed in a game is a man in the trance. In fact, watching a sporting event, especially on television, is the best way for him to get into the trance. Everything else is shut out. So if you really need to communicate with him, you had better wait for a commercial, and even then you probably should turn the television off. Or at least turn the sound down. If you turn it off he may be afraid he'll miss it when it starts again, and so he won't be concentrating on you. Halftime is probably your best bet. Even he gets up during halftime! But don't expect to have his attention for all of halftime. He won't want to miss the recap of the first half, plus summaries of all the games he isn't watching.

We have said that men have difficulty feeling sure of their masculinity. So, in sports, the strength and physical prowess, the virility of the stars are important. Those are things that a man likes to identify with. I don't know if there is a man alive who does not wish that he had been able to be a professional athlete. It may not be very prominent in his mind, or an obsession, and it may not cause him any real regrets about his life. But I'd bet that hidden in there, and not too hard to find, is the fantasy of playing center field, or quarterback, or center. Even if it is only in fantasy, when a man imagines himself playing that position, he can, for a little while, feel that he is as strong as a linebacker, as cool-headed and fast as a quarterback, as agile and full of finesse as a point guard. In fact, he can be even better than that quarterback, because he knows what he *should* have done. ("Oh, Elway, you jerk!")

This identification with strength and virility is valuable, because feeling physically powerful is one of the ways a man can feel secure about his masculinity. And those sports heroes sure are masculine. If a man can identify with the athletes, then in a way, psychologically, he is one. He is the strong one—he is the one who saves the day. It's an important fantasy, and one that all men have.

Then there is the connection with other men. Both watching sports and participating in sports are great ways to accomplish this. (Remember the example about the water polo game, the greatest moment of closeness a group of men had shared?) Just watch the beer commercials for every man's fantasy!

In watching a game, a man can identify with the players and the teams and feel a sense of connection and of shared goals. In playing a game, especially on a team, a man can have close, long-term, committed relationships with men without fear of getting too close.

Connection with Father is also part of sports. Many men have related to their fathers only through sports. And fathers connect with their sons through sports, though not always in the most healthy ways. (Some fathers play out their own fantasies through their sons' performances, and this often puts too much pressure on the boys.) But the connection is an important one. When Ken Griffey, Sr., and Ken Griffey, Jr., hit back-to-back home runs recently, they were probably fulfilling many men's fantasies about themselves and their fathers or themselves and their sons.

Men can have physical contact with each other through sports that is unlike physical contact they can have in any other way. Outside of this arena they can shake hands and give somebody a hearty pat on the back. But there are a number of different kinds of physical contact that men can have with each other when they are playing. They bump into each other, fall on top of each other, wrestle with each other, embrace each other, or hold each other. In football, the whole team can get on top of one another, and to me, it looks like they stay that way just a second longer than the play requires.

And outside of the actual playing of the game, there is other contact. There is hugging (I guess this is getting a little more common among men in general, but is still questionable), and, most notably, behind-patting. Where else would men be able to pat each other on the behind? Sometimes I watch the locker room scene after a big event, like the Super Bowl or the basketball playoffs, to see what they do. You'll see these big, powerful, virile men being explicitly, openly physically expressive with each other. It's very revealing.

What about work? Do sports have anything to do with work? For one thing, playing sports is what every man wishes he could do for a living. And it is quite a living. (The salaries are certainly testimony to the high values placed on sports.) George Will wrote his book on baseball and called it *Men at Work*. That must say something about what legitimate, important, and substantial work sports are to men. And what a fantasy for men. They all imagine being paid huge sums to toss a ball around!

And what about how often sports are used at work? Here, I mean sports analogies. They're everywhere, and, I believe, men love to use them. They know they understand each other, a little bit like a secret code, although it's not so secret. We are all becoming familiar with things like, "We'll keep going till we score," or "The best defense is a good offense." These analogies are pervasive in all arenas. They are so much a part of the language of business that we don't even recognize them as such. Women in business soon learn to recognize them and use them. Men talk about touchdowns, time-outs, fouls, and how about plain old win and lose! And in government, there's always talk of being on the president's team or being a team player.

I said that sports have sex. I don't know if you would want to include the after-game contact. But leaving that out, there are other sexual gratifications. What sports hero doesn't get the girl? One of the things with which men can identify by connecting with sports heroes is success with women. Through sports, men can imagine satisfying their wildest sexual fantasies. And the physical thrills of sports have definite similarities to the thrill of orgasm. The end zone exhibitions after scoring a touchdown have had to be cleaned up. No wonder that when a man makes a sexual conquest it is called a "score"!

And how about those statistics! Talk about numerology. There is no end to the numbers a man can get involved with. New measures and scores are invented, it seems, by the minute. The latest edition of the *Baseball Encyclopedia* has a description on the jacket that says that the volume includes "three hundred pages of statistics never before published." To me, if they haven't been published before, then they must not be very important. But that's not right. Any new statistic is important. Like, for example, "the first time a left-handed pitcher pitched a no-hitter in a double-header night game on artificial grass after a rain." And this is one that really made me laugh (and it's for real): "This has got to be a record. The referee's microphone is still out, and he's out there making another announcement. Twenty-two times. Twenty-two times he has made an announcement with no microphone. That is a record."

But recently I stayed up to see the sports news because there was going to be a new statistic. I was listening mostly for research purposes, but I admit, I was sort of interested. The statistic was that it was the first game ever played in which there were two triple plays. Okay, now, *that's* a real statistic. Try it, you might have a little fun with it. Do you know what a triple double is? I do! And to be witnessing these landmarks is to be part of a "historic" game—you're part of it if, for example, this is only the fourth time this year that a player has scored a triple double. It makes the game, and therefore the man participating in watching it, a little more important.

I think the statistics in sports are the ultimate in structure and numerology. They captivate men. They are another route into the trance. They are predictable, understandable, reportable. You can talk about them without showing feelings. You have to know some of them to be a real man. We may laugh, but this is serious business.

What's a woman to do? When you see how powerful

sports are, how many needs are met for men through sports, it makes more sense that men are so involved in sports. In some sense, it's a hopeless case. That is, it's hopeless if you want a man to give up his involvement or not care so much about sports.

There are probably some things that we would not give up, though none of them is, I think, as compelling. Would you give up shopping? Would you give up talking with your friends? Would you give up fixing up the house, trying to find the perfect placemats to go with the new dishes? Probably not. Sports are more important than any of those things, except maybe having friends.

What should Laura do about Ed? First of all, she should stop being so surprised, as if each time he chooses to watch TV it is a new rejection of her. She could do a little planning. She could ask what games he plans to watch and try to plan things they could do together at different times. They could have gone for a walk in the morning, had lunch, and been home in time for the game.

But it's not easy, and sometimes it really feels bad. One boyfriend of mine who was really involved in sports used to listen to sports talk shows on the radio. When he would pick me up for a date, I would be looking forward to an evening together. If we were going to a play, I would want to talk about that. If we were going to a party, I would want to talk about who would be there. He, however, would switch on the radio. It was lonely for me, though in retrospect, I assume it was safe and comfortable for him.

The situation continues to worsen for many women, in

light of new technology. Designed mainly by men, the new technology has given us "improvements" such as sports phone lines, big screen TV's with "windows" to allow a viewer to watch two games at once, and national and world-wide cable TV. Something is always available.

Remember, men don't feel very secure about themselves; they don't have a dependable sense of their own masculinity. Sports help give that to them. So you can't fight it. But you *can* ask for a little cooperation. You can do some planning together. You can ask him if he could choose part of a game to watch, and then you can plan some time together during the other part.

You can find some activities that you enjoy doing on your own, so that you don't always wish that he would be doing something with you instead of watching that game. He probably doesn't enjoy shopping as you do. In fact, when you shop together, he probably lingers as long as possible at TV stores, watching sports!

You can learn to enjoy some of what he enjoys. Some of it is really fun. But you have to know the players and the rules. Get him to explain some of it to you. Watch the game, trying to use some of your new knowledge. Pay attention to the sports news on television. You'll get a pretty good idea about what's important. Try learning a sport, perhaps one that you could share with him, or even one of your own.

You know you can't force him away from sports, but you wish he wouldn't hang on so tightly. If you complain less, and listen more, at least you may be able to understand more about what sports mean to him. Don't forget, he doesn't have any idea of why you would want to spend an entire afternoon shopping without buying anything. Sports are going to stay important to him. There's no way to change that. But I do think that if you don't make him feel that you are trying to take him away from the most comforting thing he knows, if he knows that he has *some* support from you, he might not have to defend it quite so fiercely.

CONCLUSION

In the early seventies, *Ms.* magazine published a short article by Alan Alda in which he explained to women things about men we really all should know. He organized these principles into the "... seven warning signs of testosterone poisoning." These included things like preoccupation with long, geometrical shapes and a fascination with numbers. He went on to offer advice to women about how and when to insist that men shape up. Since the article was written by Alan Alda, it was pretty funny. In fact, I thought it was so funny that I never forgot it. "Seven warning signs of testosterone poisoning." Ha!

It's easy to make jokes about the "others," and I admit, I still do it when I'm not in mixed company. That's okay as a stress reliever every now and then. But except for getting rid of some tension, it doesn't help anything.

In this book I've described a number of principles that help us understand men. But the most important concept I want to get across isn't any fact. It's an attitude.

We're all struggling. We just do it in different ways. If you can find yourself thinking, "Oh, so *that's* what he's trying to do," instead of "Why would he do something so stupid?" you've gotten my main point.

In the process of making this attitude shift, specific knowledge helps. The main points to keep in mind are these:

• Men are like soldiers. They have to do painful and dangerous things without question. As a result, they become numb to their feelings.

• Men are like little boys who are raised by big (and powerful) mothers. And they continue to relate to women from this point of view.

• Men use concrete structures to help them feel organized, connected, and safe.

• They often use a kind of trance, a self-hypnotic state, to block out painful or confusing feelings.

• They need other men to develop and maintain their masculine identity, which is precarious.

• They measure themselves by the work that they do.

• They need sex as an emotional connection, yet they also use sex as a pure physical release.

• Men are fascinated by and preoccupied with numbers.

• And they adore sports, even need sports, because sports meet so many needs.

With these ideas in mind, we can look at a few dilemmas between men and woman and discuss how to move toward solving them.

Arnie and Beth have finally made it into couples' counseling. Beth had been in therapy for a while, often complaining about Arnie:

"He ignores me. When we're out socializing, he's the life of the party. When we're alone, he falls asleep. I know he has a lot of changing to do, and it seems like he is going to try. But it's going to take a long time. What should I do while I'm waiting?"

Beth really wanted to *do* something. She wanted to get busy working on what was happening to the feelings between them. She wanted to talk about it with Arnie.

Women generally relish an open-ended discussion. We like nothing better than to have all the time in the world in which to thrash things out. This is enough to make the average man run for cover! (Or enter the trance.)

Beth's automatic response to the anxiety she felt about wanting a better relationship with Arnie was to "work on it." Now. Constantly. That turns out to be about the worst thing that she can do. What helped Beth feel better made Arnie feel worse. In the arena of feelings, he was inadequate. Arnie didn't know what he felt. He didn't really know what was wrong between them, yet he loved Beth, didn't want to lose her, and wanted her to be happy. The more she pressed him about it, the more inadequate he felt. His response to this was to back off, sometimes quietly, or moodily, sometimes angrily.

The more Beth pushed, the less she got. I suggested she build more structure into what she was doing with Arnie. Her nonstop, open-ended questions were impossible for Arnie to respond to. Beth pushed him to talk about his feelings, to talk about what was wrong. But Arnie had no experience with this, and when he felt inadequate, he felt frightened and out of control. He needed to feel organized and to regain control.

Arnie had few verbal skills for handling psychological challenges, such as being asked to talk about his feelings. The best way he had to handle such a stress was to block off the feelings and "think logically." In such a state he would give yes, no, or other one-word answers. He would be hiding behind the grid of his structure, and he would answer the questions as "correctly" as he could. But these felt like evasions to Beth, not answers.

I explained Arnie's difficulty to Beth and helped her see some of the ways in which Arnie thought, felt, and acted differently than she did. We looked together at why her constant requests to deal with their issues caused so much difficulty.

Beth understood. When she said to Arnie, "I'd like to spend some time this weekend talking about things," she saw him tense up. When she followed with "What time would be good for you?" she saw Arnie visibly relax. The whole weekend was more enjoyable, with plenty of laughter, shared activities, private time, as well as some serious discussion of problems and differences. "I think he was relieved that I wasn't going to be on him all the time," explained Beth.

Arnie hasn't suddenly become a different person. But he is more available when he doesn't feel that he is constantly under attack. And when Beth's questions and comments are unpredictable and nearly constant, Arnie has to defend himself against them. He has to insulate himself against what he feels is a surprise attack. When Beth makes it clear that she is not going to barrage him with her agenda, he can relax. When he doesn't have to defend himself against feelings of inadequacy, he can be a lot freer to be himself and to work on issues. He doesn't have to be so walled off.

There is probably nothing that is going to trigger a man to wall himself off and look (and be) emotionally blank more than being threatened with feeling inadequate. And there is probably nothing that makes a man feel more inadequate than having to try to deal with his wife's feelings—or his own—under her interrogation.

BELIEVING THE DIFFERENCES

Being a man is a risky proposition. A man has to earn his manhood. And once he does, his "reward" is to get to do it again, over and over, until he dies.

If you have understood this book, you understand something about this. You are beginning to understand how and why men think, feel, and act differently than women do. You are less likely to think automatically that they are silly or crazy or stubborn or rude, and more likely to think that there is something about them that you don't understand.

Men and women speak two different languages, and we are in the process of learning how to translate. That means learning the other person's language and learning about the world in which they live. When we think that men are just being stubborn or inconsiderate, we are not in a frame of mind in which to understand them. We just want them to shape up! But translating offers something different, because we not only want them to understand what *we* mean; we also want to understand what *they* mean. In doing this, we must understand them from their own perspective.

Their perspective includes a kind of grief and loss that is different from our own. We have suffered from devaluation and subjugation that have cost us greatly. And these injustices have occurred at the hands of men. This truly causes interference in our attempts to try to be more empathic to them. It is an important issue to work on. But it is separate from the work of understanding a particular man himself.

For the most part, we are trying to understand one unique man, who is of special importance to us. For him, we may be able to put aside the broader injustices and focus on the individual.

The individual man is at a loss when it comes to his masculinity, and often when it comes to his true self. He hasn't had the opportunity to have the close, nurturing presence of the future version of himself, his father. This is a loss that is different from that with which most of us as women have to deal. He has not had the opportunity to be in the comfortable presence of the person from whom he could gain a sense of inner strength and security. He has to cope with this, find substitutes for it, and protect himself from the pain associated with it. The defenses that develop are sometimes unpleasant to deal with. But their unpleasantness says something about the pain that stimulated them.

Men have been almost systematically deprived of contact with their own feelings. They develop a kind of armor to protect themselves from feelings, and they develop a set of priorities that don't involve feelings directly. These are the things that we have to keep in mind as we try to understand men.

USING THE TOOLS

Many of you find that you want to change things in your relationships with men. If you change how you relate in general to men, you put at risk relationships that may or may not be important to you. You may change how you date, or you might change how you relate to your boss and co-workers. These are moderate risks.

If you decide to change how things are in a very important relationship—with your husband, your boyfriend, your father, or your brother—you are facing a great risk to the relationship. That's why it is so difficult to make these changes. If someone is important to us, we are willing to put up with a lot, just to feel that the relationship is safe. We don't want to say what's wrong for fear that the important person will leave.

Unfortunately, what we do in the name of maintaining the relationship does not always maintain it in a very positive state. If you are resentful about what you are putting up with, that resentment negatively colors the whole relationship.

But changing it is difficult. The people with whom you are in relationships will probably not want you to change. It is in our nature as human beings to want to maintain the status quo. You threaten this when you change, and you will get resistance from the people you are trying to influence. I am not going to go into detail on this, but will refer you to an excellent book on the subject. *The Dance of Anger* by Harriet Lerner spells out very clearly how this works.

Even if you master the technique, though, the risk is this: you sometimes risk losing the relationship. I know that sounds scary, but if you stop taking care of a relationship the way that you have been, a big adjustment is required. The relationship may not have the capacity to change, and you will have to decide how important this change is to you. You may see that you must change back to the way you were or lose the relationship. You have to be aware that these are the risks. They are usually worth it. But each person has to decide what she is willing to do.

Sometimes you can make these changes on your own. And sometimes it doesn't work to do it by yourself. You may find that you are too angry to be able to be honestly objective or helpful to the other person. You may find yourself reacting rather than thinking. Your partner may not be able to listen to you. If either one of you can only seem to see the other as the enemy, then you probably need professional help.

Sometimes either one or both of you have such difficult or problematic areas from your background that you need a trained therapist to help you. This person can help explain one's pain or vulnerability to the other. You may need extended help to learn to work together. Or you may need some brief therapy to get you started and help you learn to talk productively to each other. Consider getting professional help if you are trying but feeling stuck.

This has not been a book of techniques, but rather a set of concepts. These concepts make sense out of what might otherwise be confusing or infuriating. When things make sense, we all have a much better chance of knowing what to do.

I don't really want to tell you what to do, because a prescription for one situation won't work for another. But the ideas do work. So I'll go back over a couple of examples from earlier chapters and suggest some possible ways to proceed.

Let's look at the problems Julie has with Alan. Remember, she feels that he takes advantage of her because he does not tend to household responsibilities to any significant extent. He takes out the garbage and gives himself a lot of credit for remembering it almost all of the time. He prepares the evening meal, but usually he makes sandwiches, or heats leftovers from a meal that Julie has prepared. He vacuums when Julie asks him to.

When it comes to the house, Alan is typical. Julie has a problem to solve that many of us also have, as this is a major problem for women of our generation. According to Arlie Hochschild in *The Second Shift*, women work an extra month of twenty-four-hour days of work per year in housework. When the men in their homes take on responsibilities, they often do the same kinds of jobs that children do, which does not relieve the woman of much of the burden of running a household.

This other work is invisible to men. They were not raised, as we were, to pay attention to how to keep a home running and clean. Dave Barry, a humorist who knows a lot about being a man, has a funny but true comment on this in his book *Dave Barry's Guide to Love and/or Sex*. He writes that men belong to the group of the "cleaning impaired." He says that "while women are capable of seeing individual molecules of dirt, men cannot see dirt until it has aggregated into clumps large enough to support commercial agriculture." Sad but true.

Men were never taught any differently. They will never know about housework the way that we know about it, unless it is in them from childhood. They are just never going to care as much as we do.

I believe in picking my battles. It is not going to pay off if my goal is, for example, to get my husband to see the need for floor-cleaning the way I see it. I'll tell you how I know this: I asked him a lot about it. At first I asked him about thoughts, feelings, and opinions. I didn't think we were anywhere near a resolution. Then I asked him to tell me what he saw as the minimum frequency necessary for kitchen floor-washing, and I told him mine. I hoped we could reach a compromise. My minimum was every two weeks. His was once a year!

You see, it really doesn't matter to him. It really matters

to me. (If I had lived with my husband before I put down a new floor, I would not have picked white tile!) What makes my idea any more valuable than his? Because I think so? Because I like to be right?

I'll give you another example from my own life. I felt like I was doing almost all of the tedious, everyday clean-up chores, like breakfast dishes, loading and unloading the dishwasher, clearing off the kitchen counters, sorting the mail, throwing out the newspapers. My husband disagreed; he was sure he was doing his share. We agreed that we should make a list and write down everything we did. Within two days I had made my point. Since then things have changed. But I had to find a way to show him. His perception had been different from mine.

Now, Julie has an additional issue with Alan. It's a thornier, subtler issue. The trouble is this: Alan is so vulnerable to Julie, and so needs her approval, that he withdraws rather than risk the disappointment of not winning her smile. When she is disappointed because he is not helping her, he pulls back in order not to feel inadequate. This is painful because it leaves Julie feeling lonely and isolated. But it is such a well-practiced defense for Alan that it is basically invisible to him. It looks like there is nothing to talk about. But there is.

Julie can comment on it, acknowledge it. She can say, "You seem so distant from me today that it feels like I've done something to annoy you. If I have, I'd like to know what it is." Alan will probably say that nothing is wrong, because that's how he feels. But something *is* wrong. Julie can add, "Maybe there's nothing you are aware of now.

But I still think there's something wrong, because you don't seem like yourself. Maybe whatever it is doesn't seem very important, but it might be, because you're so far away." Then she should leave it alone. It will take many repetitions before Alan will open up to this. He feels that it's a set-up. He is not used to experiencing how it feels for someone to care that much about his inner world. He will need to be quite trusting to answer these questions.

The other thing that Julie can do is to be aware of how important her comments and criticisms really are to Alan. She may be able to notice a withdrawal happening, and then she can say something about it. For example, "You seemed to flinch just now when I said that. Did it sound critical?" That is the beginning of a dialogue in which each person has the potential to understand the other better: Alan that Julie didn't mean to be critical, Julie that there are certain expressions that she feels are harmless that are not at all so to Alan.

I think that much of this sounds like extra care-taking of men's feelings, and I believe that it is. But feelings have been our specialty, and men have been out of touch. It falls to us to help them catch up if we want a more equal emotional relationship. If you don't like it, don't do it. But at least know what you are dealing with.

Now let's go back to Henry and Sue, the couple in marital therapy whose daughter Lisa had been in a serious auto accident. Sue was distressed about how Henry was dealing with the difficulty. She had been pleased by the progress they had been making in their counseling. Now Henry wanted to stop that part of their lives and focus on other things: his work, his financial status, Lisa's surgery and physical therapy schedule, and his regular bicycle riding. Sue thought that there was no room for her and her feelings in Henry's life. She was correct.

Henry was dealing with the stress in the best way he knew how. Shutting out feelings was very adaptive for him. He didn't think that he could work ten or twelve hours each day if he thought about his feelings. If he let his feelings assume importance, he would have wanted to be with Lisa at the hospital all day long and make her better. But that wasn't possible for him. He couldn't make Lisa better, and he had to continue to earn the family's living. For him to feel so bad about Lisa and not be able to do something was intolerable. He only knew how to go away and to stop feeling.

Sue was spending time with Lisa. In a way, we can think of it in terms of Sue's having the freedom to experience and acknowledge her feelings. Of course she needs to share her feelings and she would like to do this with Henry. But if she can see how different they are, she can see how vulnerable this would make him. She is, after all, benefiting not only from his continued earning ability, but also from his ability to reorganize their lives efficiently to deal with this new stress. In this perspective, Henry's behavior is a strength, a contribution to the family.

In a concrete way, Henry is holding the family together, while Sue is expressing the emotion. If Sue wants Henry to feel more of the emotion, she will have to shoulder more concrete responsibilities. And she should support the small expressions of emotion that she does get from

Henry. As the crisis passes and things seem manageable, Sue and Henry can get back on track together, especially if they have appreciated each other's contributions *during* the crisis.

Another situation to look at is the one between Justin and Kay, the couple who had just had their first baby, Drew. As I see it, Kay was so involved in her new relationship with Drew that she left the relationship with Justin unattended. Justin saw this shift in her attention as played out most clearly in the sexual realm. It was also true in a less visible way in the overall relationship.

If Kay sees Justin as not being aware of feelings, she will not be thinking about how her change in behavior is affecting him. And if he has expressed his dissatisfaction only with the sexual arrangement, she may see him as only interested in sex. Justin doesn't know another way to think about or to feel what is wrong. He has an awareness of Kay's difference with him, her distance. But he only knows how to define what is wrong as a sexual problem. This shows Kay a one-dimensional view of Justin's problem.

If, however, she thinks about what the change in her means to him, she will have a different perspective. In order to do this, she has to think about his sensitivities. Kay is involved in a very intense, affectionate, and gratifying physical relationship with Drew. Justin is shut out of this relationship as well as shut out of the physical relationship that he is used to having with Kay. As important as it is for Justin to be aware of the changes with which Kay is dealing, it is also important for Kay to be aware that there are dramatic changes for Justin.

There are two important things that Kay should do to help her relationship with Justin. One is to talk about the changes that she is experiencing, separating them from her feelings for Justin. She might say, "I know I'm not as close to you as I used to be. But I'm not sure how to get some of that back. This is all new for me, and I don't know how to juggle all of my needs, your needs, and Drew's needs. I love you as much as ever, but I realize that I'm not doing a very good job of showing it."

Her other task is to work to make room for her sexual relationship with Justin. In this area, small efforts will bring large rewards. If Kay considers how some sexual involvement with Justin will bring things back into balance for him and for the relationship, she should be able to make the effort to focus on Justin a little more.

We can think again about Ann and Tony. Tony's trance-like states are a frequent source of pain for Ann. Her task in learning how to deal with Tony is to separate his experience from hers. Though she is a trigger for his trance, she is not the real cause; it is caused by a series of pressures and events that began long before Ann was in the picture. But now that she is there, she has to cope with it.

Her straightforward approach is the key to making things run more smoothly between Tony and her. If she accuses Tony of never wanting to talk to her and goes on to generalize about defects in his character, he has more reason than ever to sink deeper and deeper into the trance. But when she says, "Hi, honey. I'd like to touch base with you when the news is over," or even more directly, "I feel really good with you. I'd like to talk a little with you this evening," she is giving Tony room to feel safe and in control. It's a matter of believing that his experience is as real as hers.

Susie's dilemma with Jim also comes to mind. Jim has been working harder and harder in order to please Susie. But Susie is missing having emotional contact with Jim. Susie has to think about the costs of what she wants from Jim. She says that she wants a warm, sensitive man. But she also wants a successful husband whose accomplishments are easily measurable by the world at large. These two things don't go very well together. Because we are used to expecting men to work hard and succeed, we don't think about the emotional cost of this success. The cost is high in terms of emotion. It is extremely difficult for a man to be a big success in the outside world and then instantly become soft and vulnerable when he gets home.

Most of the work Susie has to do is within herself. She has to think about what she really wants. She can't have it both ways. Jim is not really a superman, even if he acts like one. He is human and has limits. Only when Susie acknowledges this can she begin to make some different choices.

In each of these examples, and in every example in this book, the single most important principle is to deal with the person, a man, according to how he actually is, instead of according to how you are or to how you *wish* he would be or *think* he should be. Men and women have many differences. We grew up in different worlds. We have learned to accommodate different sets of expectations. We operate using different sets of rules and experience the identical situations very differently.

But we have many similarities. We all have needs for connection. We all fear pain and loneliness. We all feel vulnerable. We just have different ways of covering up our vulnerabilities and fears and expressing our needs. Whether we are Chinese or American, we all have to blow our noses. We are all concerned with the same "stuff," we just have different solutions for dealing with it.

When trying to understand a man, and in trying to have the relationship with him that we so want, we have to learn to read his signals from *his* perspective, using *his* language, to know what he really feels and means. There is our translation and the road to the understanding and the connection we cherish.

Additional Reading

Dance of Anger by Harriet Lerner (New York: Harper & Row, 1986)

> This is not a book about men, but it is a book about relationships. Dr. Lerner explains why we tend to get into certain kinds of relationships, how we keep them the same, and how it is difficult to change. A wonderful book to read if you are interested in working on your relationships.

Fire in the Belly by Sam Keen (New York: Bantam, 1991)

> The latest on men's struggles in our culture to find a new kind of masculinity. Written for men, it is also meaningful to women who want to understand more about men. Much of it is about the power of "Woman."

Getting the Love You Want by Harville Hendrix (New York: Harper & Row, 1990)

> Like Lerner's book, this is another book about making relationships better. It explains very well how we repeat old patterns in our current relationships.

The Hazards of Being Male and *The Inner Male* by Herb Goldberg (New York: New American Library)

> Dr. Goldberg writes strongly about men's needs and fears. He focuses quite a bit on men's sexual needs, and how these needs guide and motivate men's feelings and behavior.

In a Different Voice by Carol Gilligan (Boston: Harvard University Press, 1983)

> This now classic book describes the different ways that

men and women think from the perspective of their moral development. Because it is written about the research itself, it is not always easy reading.

Iron John by Robert Bly (New York: Addison Wesley, 1990)
Using the Grimms' fairy tale "Iron John," Bly describes the deprivation and pain that men experience, and the difficulty that they have achieving a strong and comfortable sense of manhood. Since it uses a poetic style, it does not offer traditional psychological ideas.

Manhood in the Making by David Gilmore (New Haven: Yale University Press, 1990)
Written by an anthropologist, this book describes what it takes to "be a man" in a variety of cultures. The examples are interesting, and reading this book is a way to gain a broad perspective.

The Mermaid and the Minotaur by Dorothy Dinnerstein (New York: Harper & Row, 1977)
This is an intellectually challenging and fascinating book. In it Dinnerstein explains how men's fear of and need for women leads to a whole set of cultural devaluations of women.

Why Men Are the Way They Are by Warren Farrell (New York: Berkeley, 1988)
This is one of the best books available about men. It is easy to read, uses many examples from popular culture, and stresses the social pressures that lead men to think and behave in certain ways.

You Just Don't Understand by Deborah Tannen (New York: Ballantine, 1991)
This helpful book about how men and women use language and communication differently is written by a linguist. Deborah Tannen gives clear examples of how men and women speak.

Index